SURVIVING LOGAN

SURVIVING
LOGAN

ERIK BJARNASON
AND CATHI SHAW

RMB

RMB | Rocky Mountain Books Ltd.

rmbooks.com
@rmbooks
facebook.com/rmbooks

Cataloguing data available from Library and Archives Canada

ISBN 978-1-77160-192-4 (hardcover)
ISBN 978-1-77160-193-1 (electronic)

Cover photo: Mike Danks

Printed and bound in Canada by Friesens

Distributed in Canada by Heritage Group Distribution and in the U.S. by Publishers Group West

For information on purchasing bulk quantities of this book, or to obtain media excerpts or invite the author to speak at an event, please visit rmbooks.com and select the "Contact Us" tab.

RMB | Rocky Mountain Books is dedicated to the environment and committed to reducing the destruction of old-growth forests. Our books are produced with respect for the future and consideration for the past.

We acknowledge the financial support of the Government of Canada through the Canada Book Fund and the Canada Council for the Arts, and of the province of British Columbia through the British Columbia Arts Council and the Book Publishing Tax Credit.

Disclaimer
The views expressed in this book are those of the author and do not necessarily reflect those of the publishing company, its staff or its affiliates.

This book is dedicated to my good friend Tim Jones. Tim was the long-time team leader of North Shore Rescue and is the reason I am alive today. I was with Tim when he tragically suffered from a fatal heart attack as we hiked down from the North Shore Rescue team cabin on Mount Seymour with his daughter in January 2014. I owe you more than I can repay, my friend. Rest well until we meet again.

This book chronicles my experiences on the North Shore Rescue 40th Anniversary Mount Logan Expedition in 2005. There were seven other team members on the expedition, and their stories and experiences may be different than my own. That is the nature of lived experience. This is my lived experience of surviving Logan.

—Erik Bjarnason, 2016

CONTENTS

Foreword   Cathi (Bjarnason) Shaw

Icelanders are tough. They are fiercely protective and incredibly loyal to their friends and family. The North Shore Bjarnason family embodies those qualities. I was fortunate to be raised by George, the youngest Bjarnason boy of his generation. I grew up with a crew of Viking men looking out for me. My big cousin Erik was one of them.

For as long as I can remember, I knew that if I ever found myself in need, I could call Erik and he would come to help. To date, I've never needed to use that safety net, but I knew that Erik would give me, and any of our family members, the shirt off his back if we needed it. He is equal parts tough and caring. Friends become family. Family is a bond that can't be broken.

The same can be true of the Bjarnasons' unbridled commitment and desire to help others at the risk of life and limb. There are multiple members of the family who have turned that instinct into a lifelong calling, becoming firefighters.

Erik is our world traveller. The family was never surprised to hear that Erik was off on another adventure. He started travelling the world at age 18. His parents' home soon became filled with the beautiful artifacts he collected for them on his travels. Family reunions were filled with stories – either about Erik's former adventures or, in his absence, about what he was up to at the time.

The more extreme the experience, the more likely Erik was to have engaged in it. He did things most of us just read about. I remember him arriving home for Uncle Ben's funeral with his head shaved because he'd spent time in a monastery in Nepal. I remember the concerned conversations at our grandmother's house when Erik set off on a solo bike trip from Vancouver to Mexico (with no real game plan for returning home, or at least no plan that we knew of).

But he did always return home, and Erik would always greet you with a bear hug and that Bjarnason smile. Regardless of his extensive travels and adventures, he always asked how *you* were doing. He genuinely wanted to know about your life. Erik has a way of making everyone around him feel special.

When Erik went to Mount Logan in 2005, none of the family really paid much heed to it. Erik was off on one of his adventures, and, to be honest, it was hard to keep track of them all. We just shook our heads and continued with our own lives. However, the nonchalant amusement the family members felt about this trip – one in so many, after all – quickly disappeared following the events of May 25–27, 2005.

The Bjarnason brothers (Erik's father and uncles) are close, and as soon as they received the news that Erik was in trouble, the family lines of communication broke wide open. I got a call from my father telling me that Erik was most likely dead. I was leaving for a conference in Ontario, and my dad didn't want me to hear of my cousin's death through the television news. There was no question in anyone's minds that the disaster on Logan would be national news in Canada.

It was a long night. We were essentially told that Erik and two members of his team had perished on Logan. I waited to see if I should cancel my trip so I could be home for his funeral. I packed and went to bed, but sleep was interrupted by strange dreams of the cold and the sound of howling winds. At 3 a.m. I gave up on sleeping, rose and turned on the news channel, hoping for a report.

The report that the team was safe and Erik would survive came a few hours later after another telephone conversation with my father. We all felt incredible relief and gratitude that we hadn't lost another family member too soon. I don't think any of us was prepared for the extent of Erik's injuries.

I first saw Erik's hands at the Bjarnason family reunion in July 2005. He was on a day pass from the hospital, and his hands were encased in massive bandages. But Erik was still Erik. Despite all that he'd been through, he was happy to see everyone and soon disappeared to supervise the next Bjarnason generation as they jumped off a bridge into the river (no doubt encouraged by Uncle Erik). At one point, Erik's father, Hearne, and I were chatting and then suddenly he asked where Erik had gone. We soon realized that Erik was the only adult with the kids who were in the river.

"He can't get his hands wet," my uncle told me. Then he added, "Oh, but he wouldn't go in the water."

I looked at him and said, "If one of the kids got in trouble, do you really think he wouldn't go into the water?"

We turned and ran to where Erik was, laughing and teasing the kids. The truth was, despite his significant injuries, if *any* of those children had been in danger in the water, Erik would have gone after them with no thought for himself. That is the type of man he is. It was how he lived his life as a firefighter and a North Shore Rescue member.

Writing this book with Erik was an emotional journey. I don't think anyone knows exactly what Erik went through on Mount Logan or afterward. But through it all, he remains pragmatic, realistic and, above all else, good-humoured. Despite all he's been through, Erik still always wants to know how *you* are. His generous spirit and enormous heart are inspiration to us all.

Preface

"It's not the mountain we conquer, but ourselves."

—SIR EDMUND HILLARY

October 2005

My bandages are caked in mud, but I keep pushing on, gasping for breath as I struggle up a sad excuse for a mountaineering trail on Mount Seymour in North Vancouver, British Columbia. The rain streams down my face and drips off my nose as I look at the path ahead of me. It is a clearly marked walking path. Nothing more than a tiny hill. Something a kid could race up. Not something an experienced high-altitude mountaineer like myself would find challenging.

As if to punctuate my thoughts, two elderly women with their dogs walk down the trail and nod at me. I see the concern on their faces, the way they avert their eyes. I force myself to dig deep and push past them, hoping they don't hear my wheezing breath, knowing they must.

The last five months of my life have led me to this. After five months and multiple surgeries, the bandages on my hands are caked in mud and my lungs scream for air. I am humbled by all I have lost.

Tears mix with rain and sweat as the rainforested coast that is my home claims me. Soothes me. Reminds me of who I am. Far away from the fluorescent lights and antiseptic scents of the hospital. Out of the bed and into the wild, where I belong (even if that wild is only a few metres from my back door), I breathe in the living scent of the forest, and it grounds me.

I know who I am. I know what I'm meant to be. I was lost for a time, but now as I inhale nature I find myself again. A half-empty bottle of Jack Daniels on my kitchen table reminds me of what I could have become. But this, this reminds me of who I am.

I close my eyes and hear the screaming wind of Logan. The memory of my fingers in never-ending pain as the cold burns them into stubs. The rain becomes snow in my mind, swirls around me, wrenches from me any self-awareness I may have momentarily regained. Dizziness overcomes me, and I fall to my knees, my bandaged hands flying out and breaking my fall, becoming even more mud soaked. Bringing me back to the present.

I open my eyes. I am immersed in the deep green of the Pacific rainforest. This is what I have known since I was a child.

I force myself to stand. I breathe once again and am overwhelmed by the knowledge of three things. I am on the mountain. I am in the hand of God. I am on the trail to finding myself again.

Acknowledgements

> *"Icelanders are all immortal*
> *right up to the second they die."*
>
> —DON BJARNASON

Erik

I would like to thank my parents, Hearne and Chris Bjarnason, for not only allowing but assisting me in following every dream I ever had. No matter how asinine they thought those dreams were. I also thank my beautiful wife, Genevieve, who convinced me that my story should be told to more people than just those sitting around the dinner table. She is my spiritual, financial and emotional compass, always showing me true North. Finally, I would like to dedicate this book to every brave man and woman who volunteers to help others.

Cathi

Thanks to all the members of the 2005 Logan expedition, especially Mike Danks, Gord Ferguson, Don Jardine, Isabel Budke, Barry Mason, and Alex Snigurowicz, who took the time to sit down with me and relive their experiences on Mount Logan. Thanks also to Ales Ponec, Mike Danks, Isabel Budke and Alex Snigurowicz for generously donating their photos to this book. Thanks also to Hearne and Chris Bjarnason and Genevieve Wisdom, all of whom gave unique perspectives and insights into Erik's experiences on Logan and beyond. Additional thanks to Meaghan Craven for her skillful editing and creative title suggestions. Special thanks to my husband, Bob Shaw, for reading over the first drafts of Erik's story with such enthusiasm, and to the rest of my family for, as always, being so supportive.

The Team and the Mountain

*"To qualify for mountain rescue work,
you have to pass our test. The doctor holds
a flashlight to your ear. If he can see light
coming out the other one, you qualify."*

—WILLY PFISTERER

May 2005

North Shore Rescue. The name reaches almost mythic proportions in my home province of British Columbia. Formed in 1965, this elite search and rescue team has saved hundreds of lives over the years. My story begins with NSR.

Located on the cusp of the Pacific Ocean, Vancouver, British Columbia, is a recreational paradise where residents and visitors can go skiing, golfing and sailing all on the same day. It is far too easy to forget that Vancouver is also situated beside a vast, rugged, unforgiving mountain wilderness, which is the reason NSR exists. Over the last 50 years we have been involved in more than 2,500 search and

17

rescue operations – most of them within less than an hour of city limits.

My desire to join North Shore Rescue was sparked as a child. My uncle, Greig Bjarnason, was a founding member of NSR. Greig has always been the quintessential mountain man, renowned for his backcountry skills. He would entertain my cousins and me with stories of his numerous adventures and close calls over the years. He was one person I looked up to in my youth, someone I strived to emulate. Even today, in his late 80s, he can still be found wandering the local mountains.

I grew up on his stories of adventure and high-risk rescues in the mountains. As a young boy, I remember listening with rapt attention to the stories of life and death in extreme conditions. I was spellbound by Uncle Greig's escapades, and over the years, I developed a deep passion to follow in his footsteps: to become a member of NSR.

North Shore Rescue was created in 1965 when its predecessor, the Mountain Rescue Group (MRG), disbanded. Operating through the 1950s, the MRG provided rescue services to people lost or injured in the mountains that hug the city of Vancouver. But by the mid-1960s, it dissolved and North Shore Rescue was formed as a heavy, urban search and rescue unit to assist with civil defence activities – chiefly to protect citizens in the event of an attack by the Soviet Union.

Although it is hard to imagine today, during the final stages of the Cold War, North America was on guard against the threat of a nuclear attack. It was determined that Canada's west coast needed to be protected. A search and rescue unit was created to assist Vancouver Civil Defence, should such an attack happen.

The team was trained in subjects like building reinforcement, welding, nuclear fallout measurement, riot control, firefighting, auto extrication and first aid. With the MRG no longer operational, the team was also occasionally called on to assist in locating a lost hiker or skier in Vancouver's neighbouring wilderness.

As more and more calls came in to help stranded citizens in the mountains, the original duties of the team were soon overridden so that its chief concern became rescuing stranded hikers and skiers in the rugged mountains around the cities of North and West Vancouver.

NSR soon became a leading team in search and rescue (SAR) operations in Canada. It was one of the first teams in British Columbia to be trained in a number of areas, including using search dogs to locate subjects, establishing a dive team and human tracking. We also developed special protocols for treating people suffering from hypothermia.

Today NSR is known throughout the province of British Columbia for its cutting-edge rescue operations. The team has developed and implemented the Helicopter Flight Rescue System (HFRS), which allows specially trained team members to access technical terrain via ropes of varying lengths attached to a helicopter. The helicopter can thus drop off rescue workers to help the injured or stranded, then return to pick everyone up and take them to a safe location. Before HFRS, rescue workers would have to climb to those needing help on mountains and then rappel down to a staging point. This system was pioneered by Parks Canada in the 1960s, and NSR was one of the first SAR teams to implement it. HFRS is now used by more than 15 teams in British Columbia and is authorized for use in SAR, forest-fire fighting and law enforcement operations in Canada. The HFRS allows the team to quickly evacuate stranded or injured hikers, climbers, skiers, snowboarders, snowshoers and mountain bikers in the North Shore Mountains.

Uncle Greig's stories of NSR operations continued to fuel my desire to join the team. I started on the path to fulfilling my boyhood dream in 1988 when I officially joined North Shore Rescue. Suddenly I had the opportunity to learn from the real-life characters in Greig's stories, and, of course, I jumped at the chance. I was keen and eager to join the team and willing to learn as much as I could from the men my uncle had talked about.

Because it's an elite team, the recruitment and training process for NSR is intense. Prospective members need to go through a rigorous interview and training protocol. It takes two years and a thousand hours to complete the member-in-training program. Many candidates don't make the grade and are rejected. Many of the members of the team are also trained in rescue services (paramedics, firefighters, doctors and nurses). When I joined NSR, I was also in the process of being interviewed for my coming career as a firefighter in North Vancouver.

The Bjarnasons are a family of firefighters. Two of my uncles were firefighters by trade: Greig with the North Vancouver City Fire Department and George with the Vancouver City Fire Department. Both of these men provided another source of tales that would shape my future, as they regaled the family with stories of their work as first responders. As a young man I was driven to do what they did. My experiences with NSR enhanced my skills as a firefighter.

Once you join NSR, you are responsible for everyone on the team. Members rely on each other for their own safety, so we make sure that all our members are well trained. As I went through my training process, the senior team members took me under their wings and taught me more than I could have imagined, things that would have taken me years to figure out on my own.

NSR has evolved into an intergenerational team. My uncle and I are not the only members who are related. Because the work is so dangerous, I was torn as to whether I ever wanted my own children to join (to date none of them have). Since I joined in the late 1980s, we have lost four members out of approximately 50 (that's an 8 per cent mortality rate). It is dangerous work but extremely rewarding. It's impressive when you consider that all of our members are unpaid volunteers.

For years the team was led by the legendary Tim Jones. Tim was an Advanced Life Support (ALS) paramedic and an incredibly dedicated leader. He was the guy who ultimately had to make the tough calls and was the one we looked for when we needed guidance. I was also incredibly blessed to have called him my friend.

Tim was the reason North Shore Rescue could do the things it did. From the time he joined the team in the early 1990s, he worked tirelessly for NSR. He fundraised, did media reports and worked more than full-time hours for the team (all in addition to his "real" job as a paramedic). While all NSR members are volunteers, Tim's dedication to the team was humbling.

One of the things I loved about being part of NSR was that many of our members share my enthusiasm for mountaineering. Almost every year a group from NSR put together a high-altitude expedition. We would select a mountain somewhere in the world to go climb. By the time the Logan trip came up in 2005, we had a number of expeditions under our belts. These high-altitude climbing trips acted both as team-building exercises and to hone our skills and make sure we stayed sharp. In years prior to the 2005 expedition, we had climbed mountains on 5 of the world's 7 continents. As with any climbing expedition, we relied heavily on teamwork. Just as we did when working together on NSR rescue missions, on these expeditions we worked together to keep each other safe and alive. Individuals do not go on these trips: the team does. If one member summits, we consider it a success for the whole team. The trips are an integral part of the gelling of NSR as a family.

The year 2005 marked NSR's 40th anniversary. I had been on the team for 17 years by this time. We started talking about doing something special to celebrate the milestone. The idea of putting together an anniversary expedition to Canada's highest peak, Mount Logan in Yukon, surfaced. I was excited by this idea; Logan was a place I had always wanted to explore. And it felt right that we would do an expedition in Canada to mark our 40-year milestone.

Mount Logan is located in Kluane National Park in the

southwestern corner of Yukon. It is the highest peak in Canada and the second highest in North America. Scientists say the summit is actually still rising in height because of tectonic uplifting. But the agreed-upon height of the summit (set by GPS measurement in 1992) is 5959 metres (19,551 ft). It is a high-altitude mountain.

Logan may be considered modest compared to the Himalayan ranges (Everest, for example – also still gaining height – is 8848 m or 29,029 ft.), but height is only one of the many factors to consider when climbing a mountain.

Logan has been reported to have the largest base circumference of any non-volcanic mountain on the planet. In addition, the remoteness of the mountain, combined with temperatures as low as −50°C (−58°F) (or −85°C [−121°F] with wind chill) and unpredictable weather patterns, make Logan a challenge unto itself.

Kluane National Park is a wilderness of vast proportions. It is over 22,000 square kilometres (13,670 mi²), over 80 per cent of which is made up of mountains and ice. In addition to Logan and the St. Elias Range, Kluane is home to the largest non-polar ice fields on Earth.

Kluane is situated on the British Columbian and Alaskan borders and is adjacent to three other protected areas: Wrangell–St. Elias and Glacier Bay national parks in Alaska and British Columbia's Tatshenshini–Alsek Park. Together these four parks have been declared a World Heritage Site, and they form the largest internationally protected area in the world. The protected parklands that surround it, its remoteness and extreme weather conditions mean few people live in Logan's vicinity. The mountain's remoteness was one of the things that really appealed to me about this trip. I like being far from civilization and feeling like I'm one of the only living humans in the wilderness. It connects me to Earth and grounds me like nothing else.

Mount Logan also holds a special place in Canadian mountaineering history. The first successful ascent was performed in 1925 by a team led by Albert H. MacCarthy (a former member of the U.S. Navy and a member of the Alpine Club of Canada). That expedition took 65 days to complete and months of prep work on the part of Mac-Carthy, who set up caches on the route ahead of time. Even today, you can't get to the top of Logan quickly. It takes a minimum of four weeks to summit; realistically, teams should plan for at least five weeks on the mountain.

Logan is part of the St. Elias Mountain Range, and it is astoundingly beautiful in its untouched wildness. Logan remains what many of the major peaks in the world used to be: a raw reflection of nature.

By the time of the 2005 expedition, I was an experienced climber. I had joined the North Vancouver City Fire Department in 1989, the year after I joined North Shore Rescue. In addition to being my dream job, my career offered me the opportunity to take my vacations in large blocks, which is perfect for anyone who wants to climb.

I had climbed extensively with many members of our expedition team before. I had climbed widely in the Andes Range in South America, summited Illimani (6438 m or 21,100 ft), Sajama (6542 m or 21,460 ft) and Huayna Potosi (6088 m or 19,900 ft) with Gord Ferguson, another member of the 2005 Logan expedition. I had tackled Aconcagua (the highest mountain in the Western hemisphere at 6962 m or 22,841 ft) twice – first in a solo attempt and later as a member of a team.

By the time the Logan expedition presented itself, I had also climbed in Baruntse (7129 m or 23,389 ft) in Nepal with NSR members Ales Ponec, Alex Snigurowicz and Gord Ferguson. And in 1997, I summited Denali (also known as Mount McKinley, the highest peak in North America) (6194 m or 20,300 ft) in Alaska with Don Jardine. Delani is also the third highest of the Seven Summits, which are the highest mountains of each of the seven continents.

Before attempting Logan, I had also been to the highest peak in Africa, Kilimanjaro, with Glenn Danks (older brother of Mike, who was on the Logan expedition). On that trip I led a team that took Jim Milina, a quadriplegic, up the 4400-metre (14,400-ft) saddle in his wheelchair, making history. The team went on to summit and then took Jim up and over Kilimanjaro from Kenya into Tanzania. Quite a feat, if you consider we had to carry a grown man over the course of the entire route.

Before 2005 I had travelled the entire length of the Amazon, from 6542-metre (21,463-ft) Nevado Sajama, the highest mountain in Bolivia, to the Atlantic over four years and three different trips.

By the time of the Logan trip, I had been climbing for over 20 years. Every year I would be on to the next challenging peak. When I was not on trips, I climbed local peaks around Squamish and in the Tantalus Mountain Range in British Columbia where I lived. I felt most at home when I was in the mountains. In many ways, at that stage in my life, I was living to go on the next climb. For me, mountaineering was one of the major things that defined me as a person.

In 2005 NSR had a great crew for the Logan expedition. Many of them I had climbed with before, and those I had not climbed with I knew from the NSR team. Originally, there were six people besides myself who signed up for the trip – Ales Ponec, Gord Ferguson, Mike Danks, Barry Mason, Don Jardine and Alex Snigurowicz – and I liked every one of them.

Ales Ponec and I had travelled to Nepal together a few years earlier, and he always stood out as someone who was tough both on the outside and the inside. Ales grew up in the mountain village of Spindleruv Mlyn in what is now the Czech Republic. While he never talked about it much, I sensed that his youth had been a hard one and that the mountains had been a refuge for him for a long time. Ales skied and climbed the highest peaks in Europe and around the world. He was always a huge asset for the teams he and I were on together, and he was a solid member of NSR. I found him easy to travel with and considered him a friend.

I met Gord Ferguson in 1990 when he joined NSR. At that point, I had been on the team for several years and, as we were both relatively new NSR members, we had the same training routine. We were both doing organized rescues, along with recreational skiing and mountaineering. It did not take long before we were doing expeditions and trips together.

Gord and I are opposites in physique. While I'm six-foot-two (1.9 m) and 220 pounds (100 kg), Gord is a small wiry guy. To look at us side by side, you would think we had nothing in common, but we bonded over our rescue work and our love of the outdoors and adventure. Gord and I were fast friends, and he was one of the guys I could always count on as a travel companion. And despite the fact that he's half my size, he's twice as strong as I am.

We had done multiple trips before Logan. Of course, there was the team-related training in the local hills. It is hard to find a corner of the North Shore Mountains that Gord and I have not seen. We also did some of the standard trips all British Columbian mountaineers/backcountry skiers do, including Garibaldi, Mount Baker and Rogers Pass. We also went on trips to Bolivia and Nepal. We summited three major peaks in Bolivia, including the isolated peak of Sajama (6542 m or 21,460 ft). It was on Sajama that Gord first became acquainted with one of my most defining traits: stubbornness. Despite having twisted my back at the end of a month of climbing, and slogging up the seemingly endless summit slopes of Sajama with its multiple false summits, I refused to give up. After the fifth false summit, Gord was so dispirited and hungry that he sat down on the slope, ready to quit. Without discussion I took the lead and broke trail through heavy snow to the true summit.

I am stubborn and driven, but I have never been the type to take stupid risks. I like the challenge of high-risk climbs, but I also have seen too many tragedies caused by climbers pushing on for the summit when they should turn back. Some trips do not end in a successful summit, and sometimes that is okay. If you want to climb the next day, you need to be alive. Unnecessary risk is never a smart move.

In Nepal, for example, Gord and I were unsuccessful on Baruntse. We travelled as an unsupported team, with no Sherpas, and, after losing half our members to illness and half our gear to mechanical problems, we still got through some technical climbing to Camp One above the West Col before bailing. Our retreat over the col was followed by a week-long trek out to the nearest village, and the nearest food. I had a lung infection that had me spitting up blood, but I did what I had to do: shrug it off and keep down-climbing. To push on for a summit attempt in that situation would have been sheer stupidity and would no doubt have put both myself, and my team, in danger. Gord, like me, was calculating with the risks he took.

Mike Danks was the youngest member of our 2005 expedition team. NSR is a family business for Mike. Both his dad and his brother are involved in the team. Today Mike is the team leader of NSR; he took over when we tragically lost Tim Jones to a heart attack in January 2014.

Although he is much younger than me, by the time of the Logan expedition I had known Mike for many years, and I liked the kid. Not only were we both members of NSR but, at that time, Mike worked under me as a firefighter. In addition, Mike and I had many family ties: his father had trained me on North Shore Rescue, his brother Glenn and I climbed together, his mother-in-law worked with us at the North Vancouver City Fire Department, and his wife babysat my children. Mike was excited to be an addition to the team as it would be his first major expedition, and we were happy to have him.

Barry Mason had joined NSR as member-in-training

in 2003. Barry was in great shape, with a background as a competitive triathlete, having represented Canada in both that sport and duathlon. He was relatively new to mountaineering. Logan was his first major expedition. While I did not know Barry as well as I knew the other Logan team members, I felt he was a strong addition to our team with his steady head and strong physique.

I met Don Jardine when he joined the NSR team a few years after me. So in the beginning I was senior to him on the team. But seniority on NSR is not determined by length of service; instead it is determined by your skill level. And Don is one of the most skilled outdoorsmen I know. Although Don joined NSR after me; it didn't take long until he was the senior member on the team.

Don is an exceptionally gifted and an extremely strong climber. He is one of those quiet guys, of whom you might not think anything when first meeting him. And yet he is one of the strongest human beings I have ever encountered in my life. He is an incredible, honest and good-natured man. I am so grateful to call him my friend and to have been his climbing partner on so many occasions.

Alex Snigurowicz joined NSR a few years after Don. Alex immediately became one of the regulars on our NSR expeditions. He is a genius and a keen mountaineer. He is one of those guys who knows everything there is to know about the equipment he is using. Alex is very knowledgeable about all aspects of climbing, especially when it comes to the gear. If I were in a challenging situation, I would want Alex by my side. In his day job, Alex is a respected paramedic. Before Logan we had done a number of climbs together, including a few in Nepal.

I was lucky to be in the company of Alex and Don on any mountain excursion or rescue. I could not pick two better guys. Little did I know, the 2005 Logan trip would test us beyond the outer limits of our skills and endurance. And it would cement our friendship, taking our bond to a level I didn't realize was possible.

I was happy with the team we had. They were all good guys, and I figured we would have a great trip to Logan. I was looking forward to working hard and, hopefully, reaching the summit.

Then during the planning stages, Barry came to us with a special request. His partner at the time, Isabel Budke, was a Lion's Bay SAR team member and an experienced mountaineer. She had originally been part of an all-women's team that hoped to summit Logan that season. It was a team that included Linda Bily, a climber from Vancouver, whom we would later end up meeting on Logan. For some reason, the plans for an all-women's expedition had fallen through, and their trip had been cancelled. Isabel was extremely disappointed. She had all her gear and was fully prepared for the trip. Barry asked if we would consider adding her to the team.

The team deliberated Barry's request for some time. At first, I was reluctant – after all, I did not know this woman, had no idea of her experience and, for this expedition I certainly wanted to be sure that my team members were fit and knowledgeable.

In addition, having a woman join the team would

change the dynamic of our all-male NSR team. She would be the only female on the team, the only person who was not a member of NSR, and her climbing with Barry would mean we would have a couple climbing with us. Regardless of her experience and enthusiasm, there was no question that having her along would change the complexion of the trip for us.

We met with Isabel in person before we agreed to her joining the team. She proved to be exceptionally motivated to do the trip. It was soon obvious that she was both capable and keen. Still some of us had our reservations. We were reluctant to adjust the layout of our team. But after some lengthy team discussion, we finally agreed as a group that we would let her join us on Logan.

And with that, the 2005 North Shore Rescue 40th Anniversary Team was formed. Excitement was high as we prepared to leave for Yukon and Mount Logan, the highest peak in Canada.

2   A Raw, Wild Frontier

"The wonderful things
in life are the things you do,
not the things you have."
— REINHOLD MESSNER

May 1–10, 2005

As I surveyed Quintino Sella Glacier from Base Camp, I was struck by the raw beauty in this part of the world. The never-ending wind was a constant roar in my ears and the freezing temperatures nipped at any flesh you were silly enough to leave exposed, but there was no escaping the magnificence of the St. Elias Mountain Range that surrounded us. This was a raw, wild frontier.

Thus far the trip to Logan had been uneventful. As planned, our team had left North Vancouver at 08:00 hours on Sunday, May 1, 2005. The road trip up to Yukon had taken three long days of driving through the beautiful country that marks central and northern British Columbia.

33

But beyond stunning scenery, the first leg of the trip had been unremarkable.

As planned, we stopped in Smithers, a small town in northwestern British Columbia, at 21:00 hours on the first night. On the second day, we crossed into Yukon and spent the night at Northern Beaver Post in Nugget City. On May 3, after driving through Whitehorse, we arrived at Haines Junction at 21:00 hours.

The trip was made enjoyable by easy comradery. Those of us who had climbed together before reminisced about our trips, and new members to the team joined in with stories of their adventures (both on the NSR team and in the mountains). We were in high spirits when we arrived in Haines Junction, our last stop in the cars.

Haines Junction is a small settlement with eight hundred permanent residents. It is located at the intersection of the Haines and Alaska highways. The town was originally constructed back in the 1940s when the Alaska Highway was being built. It is where all Logan climbers congregate to catch a flight to the mountain's Base Camp.

All expeditions require planning, but Logan, because of its isolation, requires perhaps more than some of the more popular and more accessible mountains. In addition to the travel arrangements, climbers are required to apply for a climbing permit at least 90 days prior to departure. As well, each climber must submit a climbing resume and the results of a physical exam showing fitness for the climb. Park officials scrutinize equipment and supplies, along with plans showing schedules and campsites. All expeditions must have a minimum of four climbers.

The precautions are well founded. When we climbed Logan in 2005, 11 climbers had died on Logan in the previous 32 years. Sadly, 24-year-old Jessica Aulik died a mere four days after we left the mountain. She was a photojournalism student and the youngest person to ever summit Logan, which she had done seven years earlier when she was only 17. She was an experienced mountaineer but did not survive the avalanche that swept her away. There is no denying that Logan is a dangerous mountain to climb.

The weather has to be perfect before you can fly in by ski plane from Haines Junction, as the pilot must land on snow-covered terrain. Because Logan's weather is notoriously unpredictable, expeditions are often delayed waiting for weather conditions that will allow flying. Most guided tours include extra days in their itineraries to allow for such unavoidable delays. Our trip was no exception. When we arrived in Haines Junction, the weather was marginal. Another team did attempt to fly in on the morning of May 4, but they encountered low cloud and returned to Haines Junction. We had no choice but to wait until our pilot deemed the conditions good enough to fly to Base Camp.

While we waited, we sat around, drank beer and visited with the locals to pass the time. We also met some of the other groups that were heading to the mountain. There were only a couple of other teams attempting Logan at the time, and all of us were in the same boat: waiting for the weather to shift so we could get to Base Camp. One of these groups was led by notable mountaineer Simon Yates, made famous by Joe Simpson's bestselling book *Touching the Void*. We took the opportunity to talk with him.

Simon is a nice guy and a very accomplished climber. He is respected in the climbing community despite his ill-conceived nickname, "The Rope Cutter," which evolved during his 1985 ascent of the West Face of Siula Grande in the Waywash Mountain Range in the Peruvian Andes with Joe Simpson.

Simon received the nickname after his seriously injured climbing partner slipped into a crevasse leaving Simon with a horrible choice – either cut his climbing partner free or be pulled in with him. Simon ended up cutting the rope because he assumed that Joe, already badly injured with a broken leg, had perished in his fall into the crevasse. But against all odds, Joe crawled out of the crevasse and made it back to their Base Camp on his own, only days after Simon managed to solo down. The story was inspiring and one all of my team members knew well. Simon had made a controversial decision – leaving his partner on the glacier not knowing for sure if he was dead.

I don't know what I would have done in such a situation. I like to think I wouldn't have left a partner on a mountain, but Joe Simpson later told Simon he had done the right thing in cutting the rope. In fact, had Simon not cut the rope, Joe very likely would never have found his way to the bottom of the crevasse and been able to get off the mountain. Decisions like these are part of extreme mountaineering and are not ones we like to talk about, especially as rescue workers.

Simon Yates, like the rest of us, was waiting out the weather. He is a professional guide so he was with a client, and they were planning to climb a different route than we were. In hindsight, our meeting might have had a touch of foreshadowing to it.

Logan can be approached from a number of different routes. Our team was heading up the King Trench Route. First ascended in 1925, King Trench is not a technical climb. Most of the route is via the glacier system and is done on skis. The route's elevation is just over 3000 metres (9,842 ft) and over 22.5 kilometres (14 mi) long. The climb starts at 2700 metres (8,900 ft) and the journey to the summit is just under 26 kilometres (16 mi). We estimated that the duration of the climb would be one month.

As we continued to wait out the weather in Haines Junction, we met a climbing group of four that was hoping to do the same route as us. It turned out that Gord Ferguson knew one of the climbers: Linda Bily.

Linda had originally planned to travel to Logan with the all-woman team I mentioned in the previous chapter. When those plans fell through, she, like Isabel, had also found a different team to climb with. Linda is an extremely experienced mountaineer and the partner of guidebook writer and photographer John Baldwin.

Because Linda's group was planning to take the same route as the NSR team, we shared our plans with each other and talked about what we hoped for on the climb and then wished them luck. We did not see them again until we arrived at Base Camp.

On May 5 the weather finally shifted in our favour, and we flew in to base on the fixed-wing aircraft. The plane can only take two passengers at a time with equipment. So Don and Ales flew in first at 09:35 hours, Mike and I followed at around 12:35, Barry and Isabel came later in the afternoon at 16:35, and Gord and Alex were the last of our group to arrive at 18:30.

The aircraft that flew us in was tiny. I'm sure the pilot had been flying that route for more than 30 years. He could probably have flown it in his sleep. To liven up what must have become a dull routine, he decided to have a bit of fun with it; I think it was just to get a reaction out of climbers.

And it worked. At one point, he was going sideways and heading right for a cliff. And I was in the back of the plane, yelling, "Hey! Hey! Hey!" thinking he had fallen asleep at the controls. At the last possible minute, he just kind of veered over, easily missing the cliff face and giggling to himself.

Once we landed on Quintino Sella Glacier, we set to work building Camp 1. At 2750 metres (9,000 ft), this would be our base for the next month. Base Camp had to accommodate our tents, a cooking area, a bathing area and a sitting area for a team of eight. So we set to work to build a massive camp.

Building Base Camp takes time and teamwork. On the first day, we dug down and made walls out of the snow to protect the camp from the ferocious winds for which Logan is famous. On the second day, we perfected our walls, and once that was done, on May 7, we started to make trips up the route to set up camps that would offer safe havens on our journey to the summit.

I was struck by the extreme conditions we would be climbing in. Even though it was the beginning of May, Logan was one of the coldest places I had ever experienced. In large part, this was because the howling wind never seemed to rest. I was coming to realize that the cold climate would be a challenge we would have to contend with, even if the weather remained sunny.

Base Camp was stocked with enough food to last about a week because there was always the chance that we could get caught in a storm. The thought of a storm on Logan made me shudder. The extreme cold, despite those sunny skies, made me believe that the stories of Logan's inclement weather were not exaggerated. From the beginning, I knew it was unlikely that we would last our entire month on the mountain without running into at least a short spell of bad weather, but the idea of a storm worried me.

Including Base Camp, we set up seven camps along the King Trench Route, and each one was stocked with food and equipment: Camp 2 (King's Trench) was at 3365 metres (11,000 ft), Camp 3 (King Col) was at 4095 metres (13,500 ft), Camp 4 (Football Field) was at 4500 metres (14,850 ft), Camp 5 (below Prospector Col) was at 4900 metres (16,200 ft) and Camps 6 and 7 were both on the Plateau at 5200 metres (17,600 ft).

Above Camp 3 was the "headwall": a 457-metre (1500-ft), 45° slope that has been compared to the headwall on Denali's West Buttress Route. I knew that this headwall was often prone to avalanche, and above it was a heavily crevassed glacier that led upward to our Camps 4 and 5.

The purpose of the camps and caches along the route is twofold. First, these camps offer safe places to sit out a bad storm. Second, and perhaps even more important, the exercise of slowly carrying supplies up the route to establish the camps allows climbers to acclimatize to the altitude. So by the end of all the preparatory work, not only is everyone prepared for a long climb with supplies, but they are prepared physically, as well.

Any climbing above 5500 metres (18,000 ft) is considered extreme-altitude climbing. It is impossible to survive at high altitudes without giving the body time to acclimatize first. Even when a climber adheres to a strict acclimatization regime, medical issues can arise. Almost everyone experiences some level of mountain sickness (over 75 per cent of people who travel to high altitudes do). In extreme cases, you can develop high-altitude pulmonary edema (HAPE) and high-altitude cerebral edema (HACE). Most people, however, will experience nonspecific symptoms brought on by climbing at high altitudes (even when paying strict attention to a correct acclimatization regime). These can include flu-like symptoms: headache, dizziness, fatigue, shortness of breath, loss of appetite, nausea, disturbed sleep, and a general feeling of malaise. Symptoms are worse at night.

When you climb at altitude, your body is working harder than it does at sea level. Your heart works harder, your digestion is affected (nausea, vomiting and anorexia are all common) and it is more difficult to breathe. The way to deal with this is to acclimate: stay at the altitude where you are experiencing symptoms until your body adapts and the symptoms are alleviated (which takes about three days) before moving on. This is the main reason, beyond distances, that it takes a long time to get up a high-altitude mountain. In addition to being a high-altitude peak, Logan is also located in the far North.

Logan was not my first trip to this part of the world. Seven years earlier, in 1998, Don Jardine and I had climbed Denali (Mount McKinley), America's highest peak. The Denali climb was one of the best climbs of my life. It is such a beautiful, classic mountain. And it was a classic climb, the kind you might expect on North America's highest peak. We got caught in storms. We had some close calls. We ran into other groups that were having their own adventures. Overall, it was an exciting and challenging expedition.

Denali is in a beautiful area that I feel extremely blessed to have experienced. And it is in the same geographic area as Logan so you might expect them to be similar. However, even though the King Trench Route on Logan is often compared to the West Buttress Route on Denali, I found them vastly different experiences.

Denali is an extremely well-organized climb. Because it is the highest peak in North America, and one of the Seven Summits, it draws a large number of climbers. In 2012 alone more than 1,200 people attempted to summit Denali. There is a crew going up about every half hour during climbing season (May–July). The trails are well marked. If you get into trouble, the rangers on the mountain are there for you. They have helicopters at the base of the mountain; they have everything you need.

By contrast, Logan is extremely remote. Only 70 to 140 climbers attempt Logan each year. It is very difficult to get to and so the resources on the mountain are limited. There is next to nobody around to help if you get into trouble. There were a couple of other groups on the mountain when we were on Logan, but other than that, we were alone. You could stand at the top of Mount Logan, look around and not see the slightest sign of civilization. I felt Logan's remoteness and isolation from the moment we arrived at Base Camp. It was almost as if we had stepped back in time to what mountaineering was in the 1940s and 50s. I could almost imagine I was a character in one of the stories Uncle Greig used to tell us. I felt it was me and my team against the mountain. Exhilaration rushed through me. I felt acutely alive.

Logan is also infamous for severe storms, vicious subtropical cyclones that build out in the Pacific Ocean and can strike Logan with little warning. I have been in many mountain storms and severe conditions over the years – weathering storms is an integral part of mountaineering. But Logan's weather made all my previous experiences of storms pale in comparison. I did not realize there was a scientific reason for this until, years after the expedition, I read a report written by Drs. Moore and Holdsworth about the May 25–27, 2005, storm that we experienced on the mountain. According to the authors of the report, Logan is "located at the end of the major North Pacific storm track along the main atmospheric pathway by which water vapor enters the Gulf of Alaska." Because Logan is so high, it intercepts a lot of the upper-level moisture. This translates into heavy snowfall and high winds.

Logan's location with respect to the Gulf of Alaska also means storms can hit at any time of the year. Severe storms involving freezing temperatures, winds in excess of 100 km/h (63 mph), and massive snowfalls are common and can last for days at a time. Air temperatures are unpredictable, ranging anywhere from less than −50°C (−58°F) to more than freezing during the climbing season, depending on elevation, aspect and weather patterns. Logan is subject to Arctic weather flows of extreme, cold weather and high winds, which create bitterly cold temperatures.

As I drew a cold breath of frost-tinged air into my oxygen-starved lungs, I had to admit that Logan was the coldest place I had ever been. That might be surprising if you consider that I had already completed a dogsled trip to the Magnetic North Pole by the time I travelled to Logan. But I had never experienced that kind of cold. It was biting. I could imagine it easily ripping flesh away. It was the fingers of cold death touching you. It was so cold that when I spit I watched it freeze before it hit the ground and bounce. I knew it was normal to experience these kinds of conditions on Logan. It has, at times, been the coldest place on Earth outside of Antarctica. At the end of May 1991, just 14 years before our expedition, the temperature on Logan dropped to a record −77.5°C (−106.6°F). The lowest-ever recorded temperature on Earth was −89.2°C (−128.6°F) in Antarctica on July 21, 1983.

I learned quickly that any exposed skin would be frozen almost instantly. I couldn't ignore it. If my balaclava got pulled down so that I exposed a bit of my cheek, it felt like I was being shot in the face with a pellet gun. It was excruciating.

But even with the cold, the climbing was fantastic. I was just loving it. Logan is situated in an extraordinarily beautiful area, and everyone on the team was having a great time. At this point our luck with weather could not have been better. The skies were clear and the sun shone almost constantly while we were establishing base camp. The weather was so good that I was starting to think we might be able to do the climb in about two weeks, if the weather held. Our original plan was that the climb would take 21 days from base camp.

I knew from experience, however, that big-mountain expeditions have at best a 50:50 chance of success, and weather is a huge factor in that success rate. As we moved from establishing base camp and began creating our camps along the route, we had clear skies, low winds, reasonable temperatures, and a stable snow pack. But on Logan the weather rarely holds for long. When we got to Camp 3 (King Col) the weather began to shift.

3 Tent Bound on King Col

"*Those who travel to mountaintops
are half in love with themselves, and
half in love with oblivion.*"

—ROBERT MACFARLANE

May 11, 2005 – King Col

King Col is where the gentler glacier terrain meets a steeper headwall leading to the upper flanks of the mountain. We arrived there ten days after we had left North Vancouver.

There were a few teams already on King Col when we settled into our camp, including Gord's friend, Linda Bily, and her team. They had arrived at base camp ahead of us and had moved up the mountain faster on their acclimatization schedule.

Just after we arrived, the first storm of the expedition hit with a vengeance, and it quickly became obvious that the stories of Logan's extreme weather patterns were not exaggerated. It didn't take long to figure out that we would be tent bound for three or four days while the high winds swirled and white-out conditions prevailed. Piles of snow quickly began to accumulate. We found ourselves having to go out into the frigid temperatures of the storm every few hours to dig out our tents or risk being buried.

I know from experience that, in general, one should allow one-third of expedition time for bad weather. I have even been on successful expeditions where 50 per cent of the trip was spent waiting out bad weather. As I went out to clear snow off our tent for what seemed liked the millionth time, I couldn't help wondering if our good luck with the weather on Logan had now come to an end.

Waiting out a storm is the worst part of expeditions for me. I've never been good with sitting still for long periods of time. I like to be moving. And waiting out a storm is boring because you are just stuck in a tent with your partner.

As the storm hit on Logan it was so cold and miserable outside that we only went out when we absolutely had to. We would even urinate in the tent in water bottles specially marked with the skull and crossbones so we would not get them confused with our drinking water. Typically, when on an expedition, we try to change partners in the tents every couple of days to avoid people getting on each other's nerves, but often it is too much work to do that. It's usually only when you are stuck in weather for several days that you start thinking about switching up your tent mates.

I was paired up with my old friend, Ales Ponec. I liked everyone on the expedition, but Ales and I got along particularly well. He is a big mountain of a man, tough and good natured. I didn't mind being holed up with him for a few days.

We talked about trips we had been on to pass the time, but even with the best tent mate, waiting out the weather does not afford much privacy. You are stuck together in a tiny space, with the wind howling outside. As well, even though you are not alone, you may start to feel lonely. While you are climbing and moving up the mountain, you do not have time to miss family or get homesick. But when you are sitting in a tent with nothing to do but wait for the storm to pass, you start to think of home and wonder what your loved ones are doing.

My thoughts went to my two children, Ariyah and Shayman. I wondered if they knew where I was. Most of all, I wondered if there was any way they could miss me as much as I was missing them at that particular moment.

Travelling had changed for me after I started a family. In the years before my children were born, I travelled the world with no cares for anyone but myself. But that all shifted once I had kids. Suddenly guilt became a part (small but certainly discernible) of my trips. I think all parents feel the same when they leave their children.

It was a tough adjustment for me. I loved my children, but for so many years I had climbed all over the world with no cares. Before family and marriage, I was a free spirit and I liked it that way.

There was no question that the climbing expeditions became harder emotionally after I had a family of my own. Leaving them was hard on me. And it was even tougher on our family unit. The bald truth is that my need to climb was one of the things that significantly contributed to the destruction of my first marriage.

My first wife did not understand my climbing. She thought that when we settled down with a family I would, well, settle down. What she could not comprehend was that climbing is part of who I am, and I couldn't give it up any more than I could give up breathing. Of course, it was not something that we had ever really talked about before our kids came along. She just assumed that I would give up my travels, and I assumed that we would make it work since it was such an integral part of who I was.

I know I'm not alone in feeling this way. Most hard-core mountaineers are the same. The mountains are in my blood. I need to climb in order to be me. In many ways it is a selfish passion, almost an addiction, but it is inescapable.

Sure, I struggled with leaving my family at home, but on the mountain I felt free and alive in a way that I did not anywhere else. And I believed that when I came home from my expeditions, I was much more focused on my family. I told myself that my trips were good for all of us. But the truth is that climbing puts a strain on even the healthiest relationships. To add to the strain, the kinds of trips I craved cost not only time but money. And that led to resentment at home.

By the time Logan rolled around, I was divorced, and my two youngest children were eight and ten years old. My ex-wife and I were not on good terms, and the fact that I was still climbing was a sore spot for her. To say that we did not have the best relationship at this stage is understating it.

Our marriage had failed, and there was a lot of animosity between us. We both loved our kids, but we could not stand one another. She did me no favours when it came to building relationships with the children. That was up to me. So I looked for ways to stay close to my kids while I was away.

One thing I always made sure I did on my trips was check in with the kids at home. But on Logan the only way to call home was by satellite phone, so the calls were saved for important business.

A satellite phone is a precious commodity in the mountains. It can mean the difference between life and death. In an isolated place like Logan, far away from the amenities of an urban centre, you have to conserve what you have. The phones and their batteries are so precious that you don't want to use all the juice on calls to family. By necessity these calls are few and far between, and when you do call, you keep it short and basic: I love you, I miss you, and, most important, I'm safe.

I had promised my kids I would call them on Mother's Day 2005. They were with their mother while I was away, so I knew that meant a potential confrontation with my ex-wife. I figured she would not take kindly to my call, but I had made it clear before I left that I would be calling the kids. And I expected to speak to them.

After being away from home for several weeks, I was looking forward to talking to the kids. Even though I now had a bad relationship with their mother, I would not change having Ariyah and Shayman in my life for anything. At that stage in their lives, I was not sure the kids knew that, and I wanted to make sure they were aware their dad loved them.

I was sitting in the tent with Ales when the time came to put the call through. I had been on many expeditions with Ales, and we had settled into an easy companionship in the tent. As I prepared to call home on the satellite phone, he turned to his book on his own side of the tent to give me some privacy (as much as such accommodations can provide). I really appreciated the gesture.

As had been prearranged, I put the call through to home and waited. When my ex-wife picked up the phone, I told myself that I would not get into a confrontation with her. I had already decided that, even if it killed me, being nice to her was probably the best way to get to talk to my kids. I knew she held all the cards.

I started off politely asking, "How are you doing?" And then before she could reply with what was sure to be a biting remark, I asked, "Are Shayman and Ariyah there?" I called to speak to the kids, not her. I forced myself to focus on that.

There was a moment of silence, and then she said in a singsong tone, "Hello? Who is this? I can't hear you."

She was acting as if the reception were poor. Suspicion immediately pricked at my nerves, and a voice inside my head asked if she was playing one of her cruel games. I don't know why I immediately doubted her motives – after all, I was calling on the satellite phone from a remote mountain in Yukon. It was reasonable that reception might be bad. But something felt wrong about this. On my end, the line was crystal clear.

Again, with that musical, almost giddy quality to her voice, she said, "I can't hear you."

My temper flared, and my gut tightened in anger. She was going to keep my kids from me. I just knew it. I took a breath and tried to calm myself. Losing my temper would not improve the situation.

After a brief pause, during which I struggled to rein in my emotions, I tried again, forcing myself to speak calmly: "It's Erik. Can I talk to the kids?"

On the other end, her voice was cheery as she said, "Who's there? I can't hear you."

In that moment I felt certain that she was lying. I was sure that she could hear me just fine. Because she *knew* I was on Logan. She *knew* I would be calling. I had prearranged the time with her and everything. So, if there truly was a problem with the connection, it was weird that she wasn't saying something like, "Erik, is that you? The reception is bad."

No, I wasn't buying this. My instincts were screaming at me there was nothing wrong with the reception. It was just another one of her ways to try to get back at me. I was thousands of kilometres away in a remote location and there was absolutely nothing I could do. And she knew it.

It soon became obvious that she was not going to let me talk to my kids. Completely frustrated and angry but also aware that I was wasting the satellite phone's battery on the call, I hung up. Bitterness filled me as I realized that she really did not want me to talk to the kids. What possible reason could she have? There was only one: to turn my kids against me.

In disbelief, I quickly placed another call to my parents, who also lived in the Vancouver area, and the call went through to them with no problem. I quickly told my mother what had happened and asked her if she would call the kids and let them know that I had tried to get through.

After I ended the call, my shoulders slumped in defeat. I wondered what my kids would think of me. Would my mom have better luck than I did contacting them, or would she not be able to get through, either? Would the kids even know I tried? Or would they just figure their dad was a selfish bastard who was off on an adventure and did not care for them? Their mother surely would promote the latter idea. And the most frustrating thing was that there was nothing I could do about it.

The complete injustice of it, along with a sudden deep loneliness, filled me. I imagined not having a relationship with my children. What would my life be like without them in it? Would I end up alone in the end? Would Ariyah and Shayman never know how much I cared?

Helplessness washed over me. They would be thinking I had abandoned them when I had promised I would call. And I knew my ex-wife would milk that story for all it was worth. The kids were innocent pawns in the game of revenge.

I slumped back on my sleeping bag in utter defeat. Misery and loneliness overwhelmed me. Then it shifted to anger as frustration seeped into my heart. I loved those kids so much. They *had* to know that.

"But how could they?" I asked myself bitterly. I was not

there and I knew their mother would tell them that I did not even bother to call. She would tell them that I did not care. And would they believe her? That was my greatest fear. What if they did?

Every serious climber has to admit that the sport can be a selfish activity. We leave our loved ones for months at time to go remote places on the planet and follow our passion – chasing the mountain. There is nothing to be gained for our family by such pursuits. We put ourselves in danger – some would say unnecessary danger. And, unless you have been bitten by the climbing bug, you cannot really understand the drive, the very real need to climb. How could I expect my two young children to understand something I could not even explain myself?

"And why shouldn't they believe what their mother told them?" I asked myself. After all, I was not there. I was far away, and their mother was the one looking after them. The anger at my ex-wife, the fear of losing my kids forever and, something deeper, a sense of despair rolled over me. I was selfish. I freely admitted it. But there was nothing I could do about it. I had to climb. Call it an addiction or passion. It was what it was.

I felt the burn of unshed tears in my eyes. I thought of those two kids so far from me, and I hoped they would know in their hearts that I cared.

My loneliness was threatening to consume me, and I was keenly aware of Ales sitting only a few feet away. I suddenly felt embarrassed. Of course, he had heard everything that had happened. Did he know how upset I was? He probably did. There was no privacy, and the emotions I was feeling were swirling between us as strongly as the wind outside the tent. He had to know how hard I was fighting to control my emotions. I turned as far from him as I could and took a deep breath and then another, trying to calm down.

Suddenly, I felt a warm, strong hand gripping me firmly on the shoulder. Ales, my giant of a friend, said nothing, but his hand was steady on my shoulder, and his strength permeated me.

We sat like that for a long time. We did not talk. We just were.

It was one of the times in my life where I was grateful for another human's touch. With the storm raging outside, thousands of miles from our homes, I had a friend. He was with me in my pain; he did not judge me. And I knew then that no matter what happened it would be okay.

4 Many Measures of Success

*"Mountains are not stadiums where
I satisfy my ambition to achieve, they are the
cathedrals where I practice my religion."*

—ANATOLI BOUKREEV

May 22–24, 2005 – Plateau Camp and the Summit

After the storm broke on May 15, we dug out and waited a day for snow conditions to stabilize. Stability proved to be satisfactory with good bonding and no natural releases. But two expeditions, including Linda Bily's group, chose to turn back at this point because they had simply run out of time to successfully go for a summit attempt.

Linda wasn't ready to give up; she wanted to stay, and she managed to join a French-Canadian team that was heading up the mountain. With them she continued on, independent of us. It was clear to me that she was very strong and determined to get to the summit.

We kept building the camps along the route to the summit. As we continued staging, we saw some amazing things. At one point we came across a gigantic serac – a pillar of ice – probably about 30 metres (100 ft) in height. It was about the size of a small apartment building. It was at the top of one of the hills, and we had to climb right underneath it.

As we passed beneath it, I looked up in awe. It was terrifyingly magnificent. I suddenly felt small and insignificant. It was a reminder of the power of the mountain. For a moment, I held my breath and I just prayed that it didn't let go. If it did, that would be the end of us all.

Luckily, as we passed under it was stable, but when Mike and Ales came down a few days later it had let go and had wiped out the entire trail. It even wiped out one of our camps on King Col where we had been sleeping. The mountain followed its own rules.

We finally got to the Plateau on May 22 and set up two camps: Main Camp and Advance Camp, which was about 45 minutes closer to the West Peak than Main Camp. Mike, Barry, Isabel and Gord would launch their summit attempt from Main Camp, while Alex, Don and I settled into Advance Camp.

On May 23 Barry, Gord and Mike decided to go for a summit bid. Isabel had woken feeling unwell that day. Gastrointestinal issues are common when climbing at high altitudes, and she had fallen prey. She was disappointed, but she elected to do the right thing and remain at Main Camp, resting. Don, Alex and I stayed at our camp, visiting briefly with the boys as they headed for the summit. None of us were up for a summit attempt that day as we were all feeling fatigued from our ascent to the Plateau, and Alex had developed a high-altitude cough.

I had done enough high-altitude expeditions that I knew when to listen to my body. I was tired, so it didn't make sense to push myself to try a summit attempt yet. I felt that we still had time on the mountain, and I knew that I could very well wake up feeling great the next day. So I wasn't concerned about taking the time to rest.

Gord, Barry and Mike all made it to the West Peak later that morning, but Mike was starting to feel unwell. As they pondered whether or not to continue on and make an attempt at the true summit, Mike began vomiting. Gord volunteered to stay with Mike while Barry continued his summit attempt alone.

Barry was in the best shape of anyone on the team. While we were all prepared for a high-altitude climb and were in good shape, Barry was a professional athlete. He had represented Canada internationally in both triathlon and duathlon, and he was feeling well on Logan. While other members of the team were feeling fatigued or unwell due the altitude, Barry felt great on May 23.

Barry went on that day to top out on the Logan Main Summit in record time. I was happy for him, and the rest of the team was thrilled. When a team member summits, it is a win for the whole expedition. Barry was the first person to make it to the summit on Logan during the 2005 climbing season (which is late April to early July). As Barry, Mike and Gord descended, we all celebrated his achievement. The NSR team had made a successful summit of

Canada's highest peak. Regardless of what happened with the rest of our summit bids, we could say that our 40th Anniversary Expedition was a success. And on a personal level, Barry could be proud that he had summited on his first major expedition – it was an amazing achievement. We were all in high spirits that night.

But elsewhere on the Plateau, Linda Bily was not having the same good fortune with her teams. The second group she had joined back at King Col now decided to bail at the Plateau, after one member made the West Peak. Linda was still determined to make a summit bid. Some of our team members were preparing to go down at this stage, but Gord agreed to stay and make a second attempt at the main peak with Linda, after a one-day rest.

Meanwhile Mike, who was still feeling a bit unwell, went all the way down to base camp. His first expedition was what I considered a success – the kid had helped a team member summit Logan and he himself had made it to the West Peak. He did a solo descent and joined Ales lower on the mountain.

Alex, Don and I planned to launch any summit attempts we could muster from Advance Camp, 610 metres (2000 ft) below the summit, on May 24.

What many people do not understand is that everything has to be perfect for a climber to go for the summit. You have to be well rested and you have to feel strong – physically and mentally. There is just too much on the line to climb if you feel off. The slightest error in judgment, or mistake, could be fatal.

Many people think that getting to the summit is the

only measure of success for a climb. But I don't see getting to the summit as the only purpose of the climb. I think getting to the summit is more akin to the icing on the cake. For me, what makes an expedition is the experience of being on a mountain, learning the wisdom of that peak and listening to elements.

I think Mount Everest has really illustrated this point better than any other mountain. Everest is the highest peak on the planet and almost every serious climber wants to have his or her stab at it. Many people climb Everest, and you hear stories about less-experienced climbers who make it to the summit. (The summit on Everest!) And then you hear about these really qualified, experienced, well-respected climbers who don't make it. And you think, "How can that be?"

The truth is, making the summit should not be the sole measure of success for a climb. Because when it comes down to it, whether you summit or not is often just a roll of the dice. If you feel strong and the weather and snow conditions cooperate, you will make it. If you are hurting physically, the weather is poor, or even if you have something simple like an equipment or supply problem, you won't.

Don and Alex were exhausted by the time we reached the high camp. Alex's cough was getting worse. After some deliberation, they decided not to attempt the summit. These are two amazing, strong climbers. But in May 2005, a summit was not in the cards for them. Their situation showed how tough it is to summit on Logan and also how the luck of the draw plays into summiting so significantly.

But for me, it was different. I woke up on the morning of May 24 and I was feeling really strong. The weather was perfect. I knew my odds of making it to the summit were good. This does not mean that I am a better climber than anyone; it's just that the odds were in my favour that day.

With Don and Alex staying behind in Advance Camp, I had to find another partner to climb with, and I did not have to look far. As luck would have it, Isabel, who had missed her summit attempt with Barry the previous day due to illness, woke up that day feeling great. So after a short discussion, we decided to set off together.

Above Advanced Camp the route leads up through a pass and down onto the summit plateau. The summit climb at Logan first reveals the West Peak and thereafter the true summit. The West Peak is the more direct climb and is only 30 metres (100 ft) lower than the summit peak.

Five hours into the summit climb, I was on top of the West Peak. I straightened up and looked around. The wind howled around us, but the view was amazing. In front of me were the never-ending isolated mountain ranges with ice fields and snow-capped peaks. I could see the Pacific Ocean in the distance, and if I looked south, I could see Mount Fairweather in my home province of British Columbia.

I took a deep breath and savoured the moment. This was what I had come here for. It felt like I was on top of the world. The rugged beauty of the mountain was spread out in front of me in all its splendour. We had come so far in the last three weeks, and now I stood on top of it all.

I looked at the true summit. To get to the actual

summit, you must traverse the north slope of the West Peak on skis, stash the skis and start climbing; then you have to climb a steep, icy slope just north of the true summit. After that, you climb to the summit itself. For some, continuing on to summit would have been imperative, but to me it seemed liked a lot of extra work for a feather in my cap. I quickly assessed the climb to the true summit and shook my head. I didn't need to do it. I felt great where I was. The weather was good. I was in an awesome position. This was the end of my summit bid at Logan. The West Peak offered the same view as the true summit, and I thought to myself, "You know what? This is good. This is what I need. I'm loving life. I want to go home safe."

I know I'm different than a lot of mountaineers. For me it has never been about reaching the peak, although I can't deny the thrill that comes with reaching the summit. But the reasons I go on the expeditions are far deeper than just a summit climb. Instead I cherish the incredible memories I take away from the experience of it all. It is a month of working hard in an extreme place and just really enjoying the challenge of it.

And I love being in extreme places. I like being on the Amazon. I like being up in the mountains. I like sleeping on crags on the side of cliff. It sounds silly, but I feel alive in such places. I feel closer to God. It is where I am happiest. At home, there will be days when I watch talk TV and feel blah at the end of the day. At the end of the day up on a mountain, I feel the buzz of life, the exhilaration of an adrenaline rush.

At the false summit, I did what I always do when I reach

the top. I left pictures of my children and a note in a sealed envelop in a Ziploc bag. I started doing that on my first expedition after Shayman was born. Carrying pictures of my kids up the mountain made me feel closer to them while I was away. And it made me feel good thinking about the packets with memories of my children in them on peaks all around the world. I liked thinking that they would be up there for a couple of hundred years or until somebody found them.

When we finished the climb to the West Peak, Isabel and I agreed to return to Advance Camp together. Don and Alex were there with Barry, waiting to hear how it had gone. I told them it was amazing. A short time later, Barry and Isabel went on to Main Camp and their tent.

I ended that day with a deep sense of satisfaction. I had done what I set out to do; I had seen what I wanted to see. I had climbed Logan. Later that night, I crawled into my sleeping bag with a grin on my face and drifted off to sleep. For a moment, I let myself forget that the summit is only the halfway point. The real challenge to many climbs is getting back down alive.

5 A Leisurely Descent

> *"Getting to the top is optional.*
> *Getting down is mandatory."*
>
> —ED VIESTURS

May 25, 2005 – Descent

The climb up Logan had been exhilarating but also exhausting. I felt a sense of real peace and calm once I arrived back in Advance Camp, but I was also overcome with waves of fatigue. I had been out on the mountain climbing and then descending back to camp for more than eight hours. I crawled into my tent that night and slept hard. When morning rolled around, I was still extremely tired. We were high enough that, while I was not suffering from altitude sickness, I was certainly feeling more fatigued than I would have if I'd been lower on the mountain.

Any experienced mountaineer will tell you that summiting is only half the climb. You still need to find your way off the mountain, and stories abound of many outstanding climbers being lost on the way down from their summit attempts. On the way down you are not only physically tired from the ascent but your mindset also shifts to "end of journey" mode. Despite this, you really are only halfway finished the climb at the summit, but this is often difficult to remember after summiting.

You need to feel as good going down as you felt going up. I may have forgotten this bit of wisdom in the afterglow of my summit attempt the previous day, but on the morning of May 25, I knew I needed as much energy as I could muster to get off Logan.

As Don, Alex and I were slowly waking up and starting to decide what to do for the day, Gord Ferguson and Linda Bily arrived at our camp. Linda was hoping to overcome the bad luck that had plagued her teams on the mountain. Her first team had cancelled their expedition before they even left Vancouver, her second team had bailed after the storm at King Col and her third team had descended after an unsuccessful summit attempt. Gord had known Linda for a few years and agreed to try a summit attempt with her that day.

It was one of the warmest mornings so far on Logan. The sun was shining, the winds were low and the temperature was −25°C (−13°F). With all our gear on, it felt almost balmy.

Barry and Isabel were at Camp 6 packing up. We decided to ski over to their tent and then continue with them down to Camp 5.

Before leaving for the summit, Linda and Gord used

the satellite phone to check the weather. We were pleased to hear that the weather forecast was good for the day. There was a small low-pressure system developing far off in the Gulf of Alaska, but there was neither an indication that this would be a problem for us on our descent to Camp 5 nor that it would hinder Gord and Linda's summit attempt.

As Alex, Don and I were preparing to go down the mountain, Linda ran into a problem. She could not locate one of her mitts.

Because I had suffered frost nip in 1998 when Don and I were on Denali, I was extra careful with my system for protecting my hands. I had taken to climbing with multiple layers of protection in extreme conditions. On Logan I had a five-layered glove system in place.

The system begins with a glove liner that fits snugly, yet allows freedom of movement and good circulation to all my fingers. I generally pick a liner that is made of material that retains its ability to stay warm even when wet. The liner allows for dexterity and provides a minimal amount of protection. I can tie my boots, open my pack, and adjust my climbing gear wearing the liners. I never take them off while I'm on the mountain unless I am really warm and comfortable.

Next I wear insulated mountaineering gloves that fit over the liners. I wear mitts over top of those gloves. The fourth and fifth layers are comprised of a pair of gigantic fleece mitts and then a pair of even-bigger over-mitts made of wind-proof material with taped seams for when the weather turns cold and windy. Over-mitts are very thin and quite large because they must fit over the other layers of gloves and mitts. They provide an extra layer of insulating air and prevent wind from getting through to the other layers.

While such a system works great for protecting my hands from the cold, it doesn't work so well for dexterity. Since the forecast was good and I planned to be at Camp 5, possibly even Base Camp, by evening, I knew I would likely take off some of the outer layers of my system, including my fleece mitts. With the warmer weather, they would just be sitting in my pack. But up on the summit, the winds could be far more extreme; they certainly had been the previous day when I was up there. I knew Linda Bily's long fight to summit Logan would be over if she didn't have full protection for her hands.

"Linda, why don't you borrow one of my fleece mitts for the summit attempt?" I offered.

While summiting was icing on the cake for me, I could tell that for Linda it was a different story. She clearly was very driven and determined to make the summit. I couldn't help thinking it would be a shame for her to have to bail out while I skied down with equipment she could have used sitting in my pack.

She hesitated before agreeing. Accepting what could be seen as an essential item from another climber is not standard practice. But as the sun shone down on us, and with the fine forecast in our minds, there was no reason for any of us to think that I would need the fleece mitts. I already had a system that was probably more extreme than most mountaineers had, and I thought I would most likely be skiing down the mountain with the top layers tucked safely in my pack. In fact, I had rarely used the fleece mitts on the trip up the mountain. Other members of the team were the same. Barry Mason, for example, often climbed with only his gloves on his hands, his mitts tucked securely in his pack.

After a short discussion, Linda gratefully accepted the mitt, saying she would borrow it for the day and return it to me when we saw each other at Base Camp.

Don made a quick call on the sat phone to Tim Jones to double-check the weather. Tim corroborated what the weather report had said. There was a small low-pressure system developing in the Gulf of Alaska, but we should be good to continue with our plans for descent. We gave Linda and Gord the satellite phone because we figured they would need it more than we would. The phone can mean the difference between life and death. Since Linda and Gord would be higher on the mountain than us, we assumed they would be in the most danger and therefore in greater need of the phone.

Linda and Gord left for their summit bid, but we were slow to get going. Normally we would get up and pack up camp around 07:00 or 08:00 so we could get a good start on the climb down. But that morning, due to the exertion of my summit climb, I had no energy or motivation to get going. And Don and Alex felt the same way. We were wiped out.

In addition, leaving early meant the tent would be full of frost from the night before. If it was still damp when we packed it up and it froze together, it would be more difficult to set up for the next night. We figured it was better to preserve our energy and get a later start than to push ourselves to leave when we were all feeling drained.

After sleeping in and hoping to shake the nagging fatigue, we got ourselves mobile and started to prepare for the climb down. It was not far to the next camp where our next cache of food was located, and since we were all still tired, we decided to use up our food and most of our fluids in a massive breakfast. That way we would have less to carry down, and we would be fuelled up. We hoped our strategy would re-energize us.

We basically ate everything that we had in our pockets, and we only took one 16-ounce water bottle each because we were skiing down to Camp 5 where we had a stash of food and all of our provisions. I expected it would be an easy ski down. Mike had already made it all the way down to Base Camp on his own the day before, so there was no reason to think otherwise. Once we finished eating, we set about packing up and preparing for the journey down.

As we were stowing the last of our gear, Barry radioed us and asked when we were leaving. He and Isabel had finished packing up their camp while we were eating breakfast, and they were waiting for us to join them. He said they were getting a bit cold just sitting there with their packs and wanted to start moving. We told them to go ahead and start on the descent. We planned to catch up to them at Prospector Col.

It was about 13:00 hours when we were finally finished packing up and ready to go. It was a bit late in the day to start, but up on Logan at that time of year, daylight hours last much longer and we weren't concerned. We thought, with the favourable weather forecast, we should have more than enough time to get down to Camp 5.

Our decision to leave late would come to haunt us. If we had woken up with enough energy to get going and break camp at 07:00, as usual, we would have made it down to the next camp with no problem. But hindsight is always 20/20. The fact was we did not think there was any reason to rush. And, in fact, Barry and Isabel left only about 45 minutes before we got going.

With the forecast calling for temperatures in the −25°C (−13°F) to −30°C (−22°F) range and the sun shining, it looked like it would be a good day; those temperatures might sound cold, but with all our gear on, we were comfortable.

As we strapped on our skis and started off, we enjoyed the view. The sky was huge and blue, and the sun glinted off the ice and snow. As we started across the Plateau even the winds were low. I couldn't help enjoying it all. I let my thoughts drift to the journey back home and seeing my kids again. It had been such a great trip, and it had soothed my wanderer's heart for the moment.

I knew it would only take a few hours for us to leisurely trek down to the next camp. There was nothing spectacular, overly strenuous, or technical about the ski down. I was honestly feeling very relaxed about the descent. The hard work had been done, and now I could start thinking about the future.

I found myself wondering which mountain I would tackle next. South America was always good; I'd spent a lot of time down there. But I had wanted to try Everest for as long as I could remember; it called to me.

Uncle Greig had gone to Everest once. He didn't summit, but he made it to Base Camp. And he didn't fly in; he had to find his own way to the mountain from Kathmandu. His journey was something I'd always wanted to try.

The cost of an expedition to Everest was the main reason I'd not gone there yet. Divorce is expensive, and I had children to support. While Earth's highest mountain was on my bucket list, I just didn't know if I could realistically afford a trip there. It was something for me to ponder when I got home. Maybe I could come up with a game plan of some kind.

The route down required us to ski down 183 metres (600 ft) to Camp 6. From there we would ski up 366 metres (1,200 ft) to Prospector Col, a ridge that marked our last climb for the route down. Barry and Isabel planned to wait for us on the ridge.

From the col, the five of us would have an easy ski down 452 metres (1,500 ft) to Camp 5. At that point we would decide whether to continue down to Base Camp that day or make camp for the night at Camp 5.

We started off just fine, but as we made our way across the Plateau Don got a radio call from Barry. He said the conditions were too poor on the col for them to wait for us. The col was exposed, and it was getting hit by strong winds. Barry noted that the ceiling was dropping, and he didn't like the look of the clouds. He didn't feel comfortable delaying on the col in the building winds until we reached them. It was hard to imagine that Barry and Isabel were on the same mountain as we were. We were still skiing in beautiful weather. Part of me wondered if they were exaggerating.

Barry said they would ski down to the other side of the col and wait for us where they would be more protected from the wind. Then we would continue as a group to Camp 4 on King Col. Barry stressed that we should hurry. He also warned us that following the wands that were placed on the col had caused them some confusion. Another team had placed the wands there, marking the way down for those who came after them. Barry said to watch for a sudden hard left in the progression of wands as we made our way across the col.

As we started to follow the wands up to Prospector Col, just as Barry had predicted the wind suddenly picked up. We had not gone far before I began to regret my generosity in lending Linda that fleece mitt at Advance Camp. The hand protected by four layers instead of five began to hurt as soon as the wind hit it.

The frostbite injury I had suffered on Denali in 1998 was rearing its head again. While Don and I successfully summited Denali that year, I also experienced my first case of frost nip to my fingers. It was not a serious injury. I had no tissue loss or obvious scarring, but having had frostbite once can make you more susceptible to future incidences of frostbite.

My hands had not given me trouble since Denali, but in the freezing winds we were starting to encounter on our way up the col, my more exposed hand, the left one, began to ache and burn with cold. I started to ski with my left hand tucked in my armpit for warmth.

Alex was starting to struggle, too. His cough had been hindering him for several days now, and before long we started to fall farther and farther behind Don, who was taking the lead up the col.

I forced myself to push forward, reminding myself that Barry had said that the weather would improve dramatically on the other side of the col. All we had to do was get over the col and pop down the other side below the clouds and we would be fine.

At the top of the ridge we were only about two hours away from Camp 4 in good conditions. But conditions were quickly deteriorating as we skied up the col. Our goal became focused: get up and over the exposed col as quickly as possible. Despite the good weather forecast, it was obvious that a storm was descending. A storm we thought we could push through, as Barry had done just 45 minutes earlier.

Shortly after making that goal to get up and over the col as quickly as possible, all our experience with storms flew out the window. We were about to learn the hard way: on Logan, the nature and severity of a storm cannot be predicted.

6 Surviving the Night

*"Mountains have a way of
dealing with overconfidence."*

—HERMANN BUHL

May 25, 2005 – Prospector Col

The wind started to pick up as we skied up the col. I saw Don getting farther and farther ahead of Alex and me as we pushed ourselves forward through the building wind. The wind was bitingly cold, and now both my hands were starting scream in pain. I started to stick first one and then the other hand into my armpits, trying desperately to warm them up while still holding on to my ski poles and trudging forward.

Up ahead I saw Don stop and look back at us over his shoulder. Then he turned and skied back to us. Barry had radioed him again, re-emphasizing the poor conditions on the col and reiterating that once we got off the col things improved dramatically. I think he was trying to encourage us to dig deep and push on. Don could tell that Alex and I were hurting.

Barry had warned that we could not linger on the col. But now that we were halfway there, I didn't need Barry to tell me this; it was obvious that a storm was hitting and hitting hard. Alex was still struggling with his cough. My hands were becoming more and more painful. But we didn't talk about our discomfort. We didn't have time. We just needed to push forward as quickly as we could.

Don, always the rescue worker, assessed the situation, got us together and took up the rear. As we made our way up the col, the storm quickly surrounded us. The snow was driving, and soon we couldn't see more than a metre out in any direction.

As I watched the tips of my skis disappear in the swirling snow, we all came to a stop. The limited visibility made moving forward increasingly dangerous. We all knew that to push forward in such conditions could mean us finding ourselves skiing off a cliff to certain death or becoming hopelessly lost in the storm. Both prospects had equally grim endings.

Don yelled into the wind to be heard. "We need to go back," he shouted.

I looked back the way we had come but couldn't make out the wands we had followed. Going back seemed just as dangerous as moving forward, and it was clear that the storm had engulfed our previous camps.

I looked ahead along the path we wanted to take and

could see nothing beyond the whiteout of the snow. I knew that none of us really wanted to go back to Camp 6 but moving ahead was becoming more and more treacherous.

We struggled to follow the wands up the col for a few more feet. Barry had told us he had experienced strong winds up at the point where he had crossed the ridge. But now that he was over the ridge, we had lost radio contact with him.

We tried to continue pushing forward but when we got to the top of the ridge all hell broke loose. We barely managed to follow the wands up a steep little hill on the col before we simply could see nothing more.

We took shelter behind a rock face on the lee side, crouching down. It was not quite as windy in that position. Don took out the tent fly and covered the three of us to give us a temporary reprieve from the snow and wind.

He said, "We need to get our crampons on and go back."

I wasn't sure about going back. It looked no better than going forward. Plus, I wasn't convinced that the Plateau would be much better than the col. Obviously going forward was our best bet, but it also looked like we might be entering a death trap if we were to attempt navigating through the swirling snow.

We pulled out our crampons, but I soon realized that my hands weren't working properly. I tried taking off the upper layer of my mitts and gloves to see if I could get more dexterity from my fingers without the bulk. The cold engulfed my hands and the pain intensified. My fingers were completely useless when it came the task of manoeuvring my feet into my crampons.

Don started to worry that the tent fly might be torn by our crampons and poles. He quickly shoved it back into the pack with the tent.

"I'm going to try to go down," Don shouted over the wind, pointing back the way we had come. I looked at him doubtfully. He pulled out his ice axe, determination etched on his face.

Don is an amazing mountaineer, and if any of us could downclimb in that situation it would be him. Preparing to follow him if it worked, I watched as he set off. Almost immediately he slipped and came close to falling. If Don couldn't manage the descent to the Plateau, there was no way Alex and I would be able to do it.

When Don made his way back up to us, I thought it was pretty obvious that we weren't going to be able to go anywhere.

"Let's set the tent up here," I shouted, figuring that it was better to have some shelter than to be out in the storm as we were.

Alex shook his head, "That's crazy. The tent won't last here. It's too exposed. We need to get out of the wind."

Alex was right. It felt like the wind was going to sweep all of us off the mountain if we didn't find shelter. To put up a tent in such conditions, you would have to be desperate. But I couldn't see that we had any choice. We needed to get into some kind of shelter before we got blown off the mountain.

Finally, Don nodded in resignation. We needed shelter,

and it was obvious that if we kept moving we would either become lost or end up killing ourselves.

Despite having been climbing for more than three decades, I'd never witnessed such a violent storm. At times I found myself on my hands and knees, holding on to the small rocks of the col. With wind gusting at 108 km/h (67 mph), I knew we were in real danger of being blown off our feet toward the cliffs.

Frantic, we set about getting our tent up and securing ice screws so we would not fly off the mountain. My hands were so cold by this stage that I could not secure the ice screws properly. And, with the temperature dropping to −56°C (−68°F) with wind chill, I knew that my hands were starting to freeze.

Finally, the tent was up. Don double-checked all the screws and then we climbed into the tent. I was hoping my hands would start to warm once we got out of the wind. The now constant searing burn that engulfed my fingers told me that I was suffering from the early stages of frostbite. Although I was concerned about my hands, I wasn't overly worried. I knew that once we got into the tent and the temperature rose, my hands would start to warm up. Experience told me that warming up would be extremely uncomfortable, but I would rather feel the searing pain of thawing fingers than the deadening pain that was infusing them now.

As we sat in the tent, I was comforted by the fact that we had weight on our side. None of us are small people. I estimated that each of us was close to or over 90 kg (200 lb), and we all carried 36-kg (80-lb) packs. So each of us weighed about 127 kg (280 lb). I figured that 381 kg (840 lb) in the tent would be enough to secure us to the ridge until the storm blew itself out.

Still there was no question that we had become trapped in the worse possible spot on the mountain. Barry's warning had been serious. Prospector Col is a 10-metre- (33-ft-) wide exposed ridge at 5500 metres' (18,000 ft) elevation that offers no shelter from the onslaught of a storm. And even though we had tried to find a more protected place to set up the tent, the blizzard had made it impossible to do so safely. Now our tent was the only protection we had from the elements. Deep down I knew that even the strongest tent would be poor protection in 108-km/h (67-mph) winds. We would have moved if we could have done so, but at the time it wasn't possible.

I kept reminding myself that a tent was better than nothing. As the three of us sat in the tent and put our backs to the wind, the illusion of safety engulfed me. We were together and all our gear was secure. Everything we owned was either in the tent or carabineered to the tent, and so I felt really secure. I'd been in bad storms on mountains before and I'd made it through. Sitting in the tent, out of the elements and together, I kept reminding myself that we *should* be safe. But deep down part of me knew that this was anything but normal. The pounding gusts of wind were ferocious, and the storm had descended upon us almost out of nowhere.

Don called Barry and Isabel on the radio once we were settled in the tent. They were relieved to hear from us again, but Barry was concerned that we were still on the col. He didn't have to tell us what we already knew: we were in the worse possible location, with no natural shelter on the col. Barry and Isabel kept telling us to come down; they didn't seem to understand that we could not risk moving. To attempt a descent in those conditions would have meant sure death.

Barry said the storm had quickly moved down the mountain and was starting to hit them at Camp 5. They were now in a similar situation to ours, albeit in a much more protected location. All they could do was pitch their tent and hope it would be enough to shelter them from the weather.

I knew we wouldn't be getting any sleep. The storm was so powerful that I was scared to take off any of my gear beyond my pack. Keeping our boots on would mean that our socks would remain damp through the night and so increase our risk of trench foot, but it was a risk I felt we had to take. If we removed our gear to get more comfortable and then found ourselves losing the tent, we would be in real trouble.

I listened to the wind with increasing fear and concern. The gusts were unlike anything I had ever experienced. As I sat there with my back to the wall of the tent, each gust of wind hammered through the tent fabric and into the back of my head. It felt like being punched over and over again.

At first we tried to strike up a conversation to pass the time. We talked about a lot of different things: the expeditions we'd been on, the people we'd met, and our families at home. Crazy situations we'd found ourselves in over the years and somehow got out of safely. I think we were trying to reassure each other and ourselves that we would get out of this one safely, too.

But talking was a drain. The wind, with its angry howling, took on a personality of its own. It was next to impossible to hear anyone speaking over the roar of the storm. To be heard, I had to yell, and my throat was starting to get sore. I would take sips of water to alleviate my sore throat, but I knew I had to make the water last. I'd already drunk more than half my bottle before the storm hit. Now I only had about eight ounces of liquid left to see me through. I came to the realization that the water wouldn't last. Before long, we lapsed into silence. And in that silence we were each alone with our thoughts.

My mind drifted to the hunger that was starting to gnaw at my stomach. I'd burned up the calories I consumed at breakfast long ago; my mind drifted to the food I would eat when I got home. If I got home.

Pushing negative thoughts aside, I focused on the meal my mom always made me before and after a trip: homemade spaghetti and meatballs with Caesar salad. My mouth watered. She made me that meal before my first trip, when I was 18, and it had become a tradition, both a farewell meal and a welcome-home feast.

As I thought about the tangy tomato sauce and starchy pasta, I wondered why it was always my favourite family meal. My parents were great cooks, and they could have made me anything I wanted to eat; spaghetti and meatballs is hardly gourmet. But it was always what I wanted, and my mom seemed to know this instinctively. For me, that particular meal and "home" are forever connected.

As I sat there shivering, I thought of the warm, happy times associated with that meal. Being with my parents, laughing over a glass of red wine, feeling the love that defines family soak into me. I closed my eyes and yearned for one more meal like that with them, so I could tell them how much I appreciated what they had done for me over the years.

My parents had always encouraged me to follow my dreams and travel. They never suggested that I stay home or give up my love of adventure. My mom would say that I might as well do it while I was young. She felt that it was better to follow your dreams wherever they took you than stay at home and have regrets later. I knew I was fortunate to have such an understanding family back at home. I hoped I would be able to tell them that when I got back.

But as the hours ticked by and storm continued full force, I was starting to become less confident that we would get off the mountain. My hands were now aching nonstop: a constant, nagging ache that was bone deep and inescapable. I took off my gloves and looked at them in the light of my headlamp. They were deep red and so swollen I could barely bend my fingers. I saw Alex, the paramedic, looking at them, concern on his face, but he didn't say a word. I tried flexing my fingers and the deep throb that had started after we entered the tent intensified. At that point I knew the temperature in the tent had not warmed up as much as I had hoped it would.

I could tell that Don and Alex were also becoming less confident about our safety. The storm was starting to take its toll. We all knew that we were in a very precarious situation. And yet we didn't give voice to our fears. Instead, we sat there shivering with wet feet as the storm continued to claw at our tent. We were miserable, and with the passing hours a dark cloak of desperation fell over us.

The wind lashed at the tent, and at times it actually lifted up the corners. Fear started to build in my stomach. Might our tent be blown off the col with us inside it? I hadn't thought it possible, but as the night wore on, I started to worry more and more. And I started to wonder if I would ever make it back home.

The gusts of wind were unpredictable. At first they were coming every three seconds or so and then, as the night wore on, longer and longer intervals stretched between each burst. As the windless intervals stretched out to six or so seconds, I felt a wave of hope wash over me.

This was a massive storm, but usually big storms don't last for hours on end. As the 12th hour of sitting in the tent passed, I started to wonder if we'd survived the worse of it; if maybe the storm was moving on. But my hopes were quickly dashed. It didn't take long for me to realize that the longer between each burst of wind, the more ferocious the next gust was. As the empty space between the gusts lengthened I became aware of a strange phenomenon. I could actually hear the wind building in the distance. It was like a living thing. It would start far off and build and build until it was battering the tent again. I started to dread the waiting even more than the gusts themselves.

At times there would be up to 30 seconds between the wind gusts. And then hope would fill me again and I would start to think that maybe it was over. We'd been in the tent for more than 14 hours. But as night passed into day, I realized it was not over. It was not even close to being over.

Our gear was top quality. Alex made sure of that. But a pessimistic voice deep inside reminded me that no matter how well built they are, tents are not designed for the kind of sustained punishment we were facing. The terrible thought crept into my mind that the tent was not going to last much longer unless the storm let up.

Still, I just kept telling myself that there was no way a storm this powerful would last very long. I'd definitely experienced some long storms that halted expeditions and confined us to our tents for days at a time. But generally speaking those storms didn't have the energy of this storm. They dumped a ton of snow and had some mild winds but not the 108-km/h (67-mph) winds we were presently battling. It just didn't make sense that a storm could be so strong and at the same time last for so long. I reasoned that it would have had to be a huge system, and the weather reports had not indicated that anything of the sort was brewing.

I kept telling myself that once the storm died down, all we would have to do was pack up and trek down to camp. Sure, it might be a tough trek in the deep, fresh snow, but once the storm subsided we would be fine.

This soon became my mantra. "The storm will blow itself out. The storm will blow itself out." Once that happened, we would just ski down to camp and join Barry and Isabel, where all our food and fluids were stashed.

The longer I waited for an indication that the storm was weakening, the more I started thinking about the camp Barry and Isabel were at. In my mind, it started to take on resort-like qualities. "Hang in there," I told myself. "A comfy resort is only two hours away." All we had to do was outlast the storm.

7 Goodbye

*"Identifying and overcoming
natural fear is one of the pleasing
struggles intrinsic to climbing."*

—ALEX LOWE

May 26, 2005 – Prospector Col

I was optimistic when we safely made it through the night. I figured that it was now just a matter of time before the winds slowed and we could pack up. But I was facing another problem, one I couldn't ignore any longer: my hands.

The pain in my hands was not receding at all. In fact, it was intensifying. I'd seen Alex looking at my hands earlier, and I knew they looked bad. The truth was they *were* bad. I was suffering from first-degree frostbite. My hands hurt, and they were mildly itchy. I knew what frost nip felt like, but I was starting to worry that this time my hands were worse than they'd been on Denali.

I had hoped that when we got out of the wind and into

85

the tent my hands would warm up. But they hadn't. They were still very cold, and they ached constantly. I didn't think they were freezing more at this stage, but they sure weren't getting better. And I wasn't sure about how much I could use them. Hours earlier they had been useless for securing the ice screws – Don had redone all the ones I worked on. I knew I needed to get off the mountain and warm my hands up properly.

Alex glanced over at my hands periodically. He didn't say a word, but he was a paramedic and a rescue worker, and I knew he recognized what was happening. Every time he looked at them my stomach would sink a little. Thankfully he kept his mouth shut, and I did the same. I tried to ignore it. I reminded myself that things could be worse.

Drawing on my optimistic nature, I thought of all the things we had on our side. We were sheltered from the storm in our tent, and we were together. In a strange way, I kind of felt safe. It was crazy, but I could feel a sense of something akin to contentment coming over me. I couldn't deny that it was nice to be inside, feeling relatively safe from the raging storm outside and with two people I counted as good friends.

I was starting to feel a touch euphoric. I've always been the type of person who likes being in extreme environments. Well, there was no denying that this was probably the most extreme environment I had ever faced. If it weren't for the constant throbbing of my hands, I think I could have said I was actually enjoying myself. It was crazy but true.

But the euphoria didn't last long. Soon, it was replaced

by sheer terror of what I was facing. If I was honest with myself, I had to admit that I was scared. I knew that if the tent ripped apart, we would be in huge trouble. There were no places to hide on the col, and the tent was keeping us alive. It was horrifying to think that my life hinged on just a thin layer of nylon and a zipper. And even though my hands were throbbing, I knew they would be a million times worse if I was out in the storm, exposed to the elements.

The storm continued to show no signs of abating. I knew things were not looking good.

Thankfully, we were still in radio contact with Barry and Isabel. We had lost contact with them while we were exposed on the col but regained a connection once we got into the tent. We told them we were in trouble, and they were already very aware of how grave the situation was. They were also being assaulted by the storm on a far more protected part of the mountain. I think they could hardly believe that we could be weathering this storm, exposed as we were, on the col.

As the night passed into day, and the storm continued to ravage us, our message changed from us telling them we were in trouble to telling them: no, we're in REAL trouble. As time ticked by my optimism began to fade, and I soon found myself starting to prepare for the worst-case scenario: our deaths on the mountain. I just didn't see how we could last much longer, as the tent was now being lifted off the ground at regular intervals. Don and Alex were coming to the same grave conclusion.

We started to relay our coordinates to Barry and Isabel. As rescue workers, we all knew that it was important to be prepared. And we wanted them to at least know where our bodies would be if we did not survive.

As the blizzard continued to rage, Don gave Barry the final messages he had for his family.

My heart sank. The longer we were stuck on the ridge in the storm, the less likely our tent would survive. Once the tent was gone I knew it would not be long before we would all be dead. If the tent didn't survive, we wouldn't survive.

I knew Don had done the right thing. If I died here, I wanted the people at home to know how much I loved them. But I felt sick thinking about what I would tell the ones I was leaving behind. As a first responder, I have seen many people die in many different ways, and often they do not have a chance to say goodbye. So I tried to tell myself that I was lucky that I could send a message home. But at the same time, the last thing I wanted to do was to say goodbye to my children. Still, I had no choice. The only other option was to not leave a goodbye message, and that would be worse. As I struggled to think about what I wanted my family to hear, I told Isabel that if it came down to it, I would prefer my body to be left on the mountain. I did not want to put rescuers' lives at risk to find my shell of a body. As far as I was concerned, once I was dead, I would be gone. I have no attachment to the physical body I am in.

I thought about Shayman and Ariyah, and the one thing I wanted them to know. Then I did the hardest thing I've ever done in my life. I asked Isabel to tell my kids that I loved them. If they remembered nothing else about me as their dad, I wanted them to know that I loved them.

Then I thought about my parents, and my heart ached. Guilt filled me as I considered what I was doing to them. I knew this would almost kill them both. Parents should not have to experience their children's deaths. Outliving our children goes against everything that feels natural to us as a species.

I knew my parents would be stunned by the news. I remembered the talk we'd had before I left for Logan, and I knew they had expected me to have a good time. I had explained to them that Logan was not a technical climb. They'd been happy that for once one of my expeditions was in Canada and relatively close to home. My dad was probably imagining me and the rest of the team sitting on the top of Logan, drinking beers. This would come as a total shock.

I told them to tell my parents that I was so sorry.

And then I started to think about another person: Joline.

Joline is my first child through an earlier relationship, but I had never had the chance to meet her. It was the one real regret I had in my life at that point.

Seventeen years before Logan, I had been in a relationship with a beautiful girl named Davina. Partway through our relationship I had the opportunity to go on a five-month biking trip to Mexico – one of my first really big adventures. We were young and neither of us was ready to commit to the other. Rather than try a long-distance relationship that would be doomed from the start (I would be out of contact with civilization for most of the time I was away), we parted ways amicably. This was in the days before Internet and cell phones, so keeping in touch over long distances was a challenge.

When I returned home, months later, I received a call from Davina telling me that she had good news and bad news. The good news was that while I was away she had given birth to a healthy baby girl and the baby was mine. The bad news for me was that she had met someone else while I was gone and it was serious. She was planning on getting married, and her fiancé wanted to make sure I was not going to be popping into their lives.

I was young and single at the time, and I agreed, maybe a little too readily, to leave them alone. Always impulsive, I did not really consider exactly what it would mean for me to have a daughter out there, a part of me but someone I would never have a relationship with.

We had always agreed that when Joline turned 18, her mother would give her my contact information and, if she wanted, she would be able to look me up. I had carried a worn baby picture in my wallet for years. I had taken it out so many times, it was so faded and wrinkled that you could hardly make out the little girl in the photo anymore.

But long ago I had memorized her face; with her bright blue eyes and pale blond hair, her resemblance to my side of the family was uncanny. If I'd ever had any doubts in my mind that she was my flesh and blood, that picture of her had erased them. She looked so much like me. At least, she had as a toddler. I wondered what she looked like now. I choked back a sob as I realized I might never find out.

I always thought I would have time on my side, that I would be able to forge a relationship with my daughter sometime in the future. But now, with death staring me in the face, I realized I might never get to meet Joline. I might not have any future ahead of me.

The realization was crushing. All the things I'd planned, all my hopes and dreams, were they really ending here on this mountain in this storm?

I radioed down to Barry and Isabel again. Choking back emotion, I asked them to find the daughter that I had never met and to let her know that I had always thought about her and loved her.

As a final message, I said, "Give my love to my family." Pushing back emotion, I struggled to add, "It was nice travelling with you."

After that it was silent in the tent, except for the unrelenting roar of the wind. My feelings were rolling with the wind. We had gotten ourselves into a world of trouble, and with the storm still raging outside our small shelter, nobody would be able to help us.

The closest people to us were Linda Bily and Gord Ferguson. We figured they weren't far away, depending on how they had fared on their summit bid. I thought of my friend Gord's easy smile and sharp wit. I prayed they had made it back to camp before the storm hit. I could only imagine how brutal the wind would be at the summit.

Deep down I had an uncanny feeling that they were safe. I knew that Gord would not have pushed on to the summit if he had seen the storm coming. And up where he was, he would have had more warning of an impending storm than we did. No, I told myself firmly. Gord and Linda would be safe on the Plateau.

Even though Linda and Gord were not very far away, we had no way to contact them. Our radios required a clear line of sight to function correctly, and Gord and Linda were behind a rock band on the Plateau. They might as well have been on the other side of the planet. They could have had no idea that we were in trouble. In the best-case scenario, they were up there, surviving the storm by themselves, hunkered down and waiting it out. The Plateau was much more sheltered than the exposed col. But with this storm, there was no guarantee they were safe.

Don, Alex and I had been on many expeditions together. We had climbed together on trips to the Amazon, Nepal, and Denali. We had been in tough situations before. Don and I had climbed many local mountains together in the Vancouver area, but none of them were really massive. Those trips consisted of intermediate-level hikes and climbs in the Tantalus Range. But we had also climbed Denali together, and we had survived a dire situation on that mountain.

During that climb we had also been caught in a storm. It was an 11-day storm above 6000 metres (19,685 ft). We weathered that storm in a sheltered camp, so we were safe. We could have stayed there indefinitely, except for one huge problem: supplies started to run low. We were almost completely out of food at the end. All we had was a handful of nuts each to live on for a week, a handful of nuts and a little bit of snow. I was in serious trouble. My blood sugar level was so low by the end of the storm that I was unable to move. I could barely stand up.

With few options, Don took charge. He said, "Okay, you stay here."

And then he did something that I would have thought was impossible. He soloed down to Football Field at 5944 metres (19,500 ft), packed up a ton of food and came back up. If I was not there to witness it, I would not have believed such a feat was possible. It is a difficult climb to do with a climbing partner, but to solo it seemed almost impossible.

When Don came back up, we ate and ate and ate. We gorged ourselves until we could not eat any more. Then the next day, we executed a successful summit attempt from our camp to the peak at 6168 metres (20,237 ft). I went from thinking I was in real trouble to summiting the highest peak in North America. All we needed was some food and a shift in the weather and we were good to go. My experience on Denali made me realize how circumstance and fate can determine success or failure on a mountain, even for the most well-trained, prepared and experienced climbers. That experience also reinforced for me how quickly things can change on high-altitude climbs.

Don had bailed me out on Denali, and we had helped Alex in Nepal when he became snow blind on one of the glaciers. We had to guide him down the mountain. He held my shoulder and used his ski pole to navigate the ice.

Remembering these times of trouble, I was able to convince myself that we had overcome bad situations before. But I couldn't deny the situation on Mount Logan was much direr. As the morning wore on, we once again lost radio contact with Barry. And as noon approached, just as I thought it could not possibly get much worse, I started to hear what I had been dreading throughout the night.

Our tent, never made to withstand such punishment, was starting to disintegrate.

8   A Ferocious Wind

> *"I have something inside me that*
> *makes me have no interest in playing for*
> *low stakes. For me it is the high bid or*
> *nothing. That's what fires me."*
>
> —JERZY KUKUCZKA

May 26, 2006 – Prospector Col

The ripping and tearing of the tent was a horrifying sound that I could hear clearly, even over the roar of the storm. Maybe the sound seemed clear because I had been dreading it all night. Maybe subconsciously I was listening for it. Whatever the reason, I immediately knew exactly what was happening. The tent, which had been our shelter and held us safe for 20 hours, was now coming apart.

I could feel the gusts of wind blowing through the seams, and soon I could see the cracks in them. And those cracks were just getting bigger and bigger with each gust. If we lost the tent, there was no other shelter. And with a sinking heart, I admitted to myself that our chances of surviving a storm of this magnitude in the open on Logan were next to nothing.

Even as our shelter fell apart, another serious problem presented itself. All of us had run out of fluids. Each of us had consumed all of our water – each of us had left the Plateau with a 16-ounce water bottle – even though we had rationed ourselves as we sat in the tent. Just before the tent started to tear, I'd finished the last few drops in my bottle.

Dehydration is a real concern when you climb high-altitude mountains. Every time you breathe, you breathe out moisture, so you have to drink a lot of fluids. The higher you go and the colder it is, the more fluids you need.

We all knew that we needed to drink and our water bottles were not going to last long. So, the night before, when we had gone into the tent, we had brought a bag full of snow with us to melt. This strategy had worked for me in the past. Usually the snow softens up a bit and then you can melt it over your stove. But when I checked on the bag of snow I saw what I already expected, based on how cold my hands still were. The snow was rock hard. The tent hadn't warmed up at all overnight.

Normally, I would have just fired up my stove and melted the snow. But because we believed we would make it back to camp easily under sunny skies the day before, I had not brought much fuel for the stove with me. Fuel is heavy, and we were all fatigued. We had lightened our loads, hoping to conserve energy.

My mouth was parched, and it was difficult to talk. There was no question in my mind that dehydration was going to be a problem. My thoughts began to focus on two things: how incredibly thirsty I was and how much my hands were hurting. The pain in my hands increased with each hour. I didn't talk about it because there was nothing we could do. There was no way of warming ourselves. Don and Alex were in just as much discomfort as I was. There was no point in complaining.

With the tent coming apart at the seams, our options narrowed to one. We needed a replacement for the tent. It was obvious that we could not sit and wait out the storm anymore. We needed to have water and to build some kind of shelter.

My hands were agonizingly cold. They were now less red but still extremely stiff and swollen. I was having trouble using them.

"We need to build a snow cave," Alex said.

Don nodded.

I shook my head at them. "I don't think I can hold a shovel," I admitted. It was the first time I voiced aloud how bad my hands were.

"Why don't you melt the snow?" Don gestured toward the bag I'd been examining a few minutes earlier. "We will start on the cave."

It sounded logical. I had my stove, and I did have a small amount of fuel. While they dug the cave, I could melt us some water and we could try to rehydrate and warm up in the cave.

There was no time to waste. Without any more discussion, each of us got to work.

I took the stove and put it in my lap in front of me. I dumped the snow in a pot, got the pot all ready and then I prepared to prime the stove. That's when I realized that in order to get my hands working enough to prime it, I would have to take the top two layers of my gloves off. There was just no way I would have had enough dexterity to light the stove with all the layers of gloves on, especially when they were already so swollen and sore.

To ready the stove, I had to pump it 30 times, twist it, light it, twist it, turn it off and then I would be good to go. That was all I had to do, and then I could put my mitts back on. So I put my outer layers of gloves in my lap and I started to prime the stove.

This simple act would prove to be a critical mistake. In my state of exhaustion, I put my top two layers of gloves in my lap instead of securing them to my body. It was a careless, stupid move – one that I regret to this day. When you climb in these kinds of conditions, you know that the cardinal rule of climbing is that every piece of equipment should be either secured to you or secured to the tent. And there were my gloves, loose, in my lap.

My judgment was clouded. I was focused on our need for water. Thirst was threatening to choke me. I needed to somehow get some liquids into us. The best way to do that would be to get the stove lit as quickly as possible and melt our stash of snow.

While I focused on the stove, Don stepped out of the tent and walked around behind it to check on the ice screws and try to get an idea of how much longer our shelter was going to last.

As Alex went to follow him, the unthinkable happened. Alex had one foot in the tent and one foot out to follow

Don. He was just about to unhook the snow shovel so they could go build a snow cave, when a rogue gust of wind hit. This was probably one of the stronger gusts we experienced, well over 120 km/h (75 mph), and instead of 400 kilograms (900 lb) anchoring the tent to the ground, only a little over a third of that weight was holding it down. My pack and I weigh in at 145 kilograms (320 lb); it was not enough weight to hold the tent to the ground.

A sickening ripping sound rang out, and the tent was wretched from the ice screws and picked up by the wind. There was no time to think. One minute I was priming the stove, and the next minute I was inside a tent that was tumbling toward the cliff.

It was a surreal feeling. My mind screamed at me, "Wake up! This can't be real, just wake up!" I was tossed upside down in the air. I lost all sense of direction. By some twist of fate, the open door of the tent saved me from going over the edge of the col with all our gear. Almost as soon as I had been lifted up, I was dumped out of the tent along with a smattering of gear.

It all happened in the blink of an eye. Alex had been pushed over by the burst of wind, but as he scrambled to his feet, he tried to grab for the tent. I reached for the tent, too. For a moment we were both holding the tent, and I thought we would hold on, that we had it. Then another blast of wind struck, and the tent, with all our packs, snow shovels, the stove, and the rest of our gear, was gone. It flew off the cliff into oblivion. Only our skis remained where the tent had been, jammed down safely in the snow, anchored there.

The seriousness of the situation hit me immediately. We had no shelter, no fuel to make water and had lost important gear. All that had escaped the tent were two sleeping bags, one sleeping mat and a pot lid. I looked at the meagre supplies on the ground at my feet and wondered if this could get any worse.

Then Alex stared at me with a strange expression on his face.

"Erik!" he shouted.

I looked at him, thinking he was just upset by the loss of our gear.

Then he bellowed at me as if I were deaf, "Erik! Where are your gloves?"

I looked down with a sinking feeling. Dread filled me as I realized that my two outer layers of gloves were gone. I remembered taking them off in the tent. Taking them off and not securing them to myself.

I wondered how I could have made a mistake like that. Now I was only wearing two sets of gloves – the lining and the second layer – not even my big mitts.

The next decision was made in a matter of seconds because our lives were on the line and we could not just stand around and have a discussion about what to do. We looked at each other and knew what had to happen next. Don and Alex *had* to go and build the snow cave. My hands, already suffering from frostbite before the tent blew away, could only get worse. I would be useless at building the shelter.

One thing to understand is that Don, Alex and I are more than just friends. They are like brothers to me. Any of us would give up his life for the other. With that one exchange of glances between us we all knew what had to happen. They had to go and leave me behind.

Looking back, I know it must have been tough for them to leave me there because they knew I did not have a very good chance of survival. All of us are experienced rescue workers. Alex and I are first responders. We know what frostbite does. This was one time when knowing so much made a tough decision easier. I was the weak link; they could not help me. If they had tried to drag me along, I would have slowed them down. Our only chance of survival was to try to build a snow cave, and every second counted. We did not even take the time to say goodbye.

Alex picked up one of the sleeping bags and wrapped it around my shoulders. Don looked at me steadily and said, "We'll come back for you if we can."

Then Don and Alex were gone. I was alone with the storm.

9 Frozen in Place

*"Life can deal you an amazing
hand. Do you play it steady, bluff
like crazy or go all in?"*

—JOE SIMPSON

May 26, 2005 – Prospector Col

I knew I needed to find some kind of rudimentary shelter
and find it fast. But on that tiny ridge there was no shelter
to speak of. Panic threatened to take over, but then, oddly,
a feeling of calm came over me. There had to be something
better than standing exposed in the wind, as I currently
was doing, I told myself.

I looked around. Visibility was worse than it had been
the day before. I couldn't see my hand in front of my face.
So I got down on all fours and started to crawl, inching
forward and peering through the storm, hoping I would
see something that I could use as a rudimentary shelter.

The storm had not eased at all. The snow was still

swirling all around me, and the wind continued to tug at me, threatening to send me off the mountain after our tent and supplies. The calm evaporated and a sense of hopelessness overcame me again as I peered through the darkness and snow. I saw nothing that I could use for shelter. Nothing at all.

After 15 minutes, I stopped, utterly defeated. Sitting there in the open guaranteed that I wouldn't survive for very long. I desperately needed something that I could use for shelter. An outcropping or even a single rock. I peered through the snow, and all I saw was white. I crawled forward a couple more feet and paused, squinting ahead again. And then, just when I was ready to give up completely, I saw what I thought was an outline of something on the ground.

I inched toward it and discovered the shape was a medium-sized rock. It was about the size of a small patio table in diameter but it was only about a foot or two off the ground. Wide but short. At six-foot-two (1.9 m) and about 220 pounds (100 kg), I could not completely hide behind it. The best I could do was to wedge myself partially beneath it.

I worked to get beneath the rock as much as possible. Once there, I found the rock helped more than I expected. I had been able to get partly beneath the rock, and the wind gusted over top of it, missing me for the most part. The wind was cut off by this little piece of the mountain. As crazy as it sounds, I was suddenly filled with gratitude for the small boulder.

But even with the rock providing some shelter, every

now and then a big gust of wind would come and lift me right off the ground. I took to holding onto the rock with my aching hands. I was terrified that I would be ripped from beneath it and tossed off the mountain by the gusts. I had never been in a wind so strong. It was like being in a hurricane.

As the gusts continued, I held tightly onto the rock. Sometimes my legs would be lifted up by a blast of wind. Amazingly, I was somehow able to hang on to the rock despite my damaged, frostbitten fingers.

It took me a few gusts to figure out why I was able to maintain my hold on the rock. I believed that with my hands so damaged already (and no doubt getting worse the longer I was out in the storm) my ability to grasp anything would be hindered. And yet I was able to hold on through the vicious bursts of wind. It didn't make sense. Then I realized that my gloves had frozen to the rock, attaching me to it.

I knew this was not good. A little voice in my head told me that it has got to be pretty bad for your hands to actually freeze so solidly to a surface that you are secured to it through gale-force winds.

I was terrified. When the tent blew away, I thought that was it. I truly expected that it would only be a matter of time now before we all perished. I felt like I had pulled my parachute cord and nothing had come out.

But even as waves of hopelessness washed over me, I still had an unquenchable desire to live burning within me. I wanted it so badly. I have an extremely strong survival instinct. I've been known to say that I'm like a cockroach; it would be tough to kill me. I don't know why this is the case, but it is just one of those things I was born with.

And so, despite my frozen hands, I did everything I could to give myself the best chance for survival. I started falling back on my SAR training, mentally listing all the things I needed to do if I wanted to live. Hydration and calories were foremost. I knew my mind was beginning to drift, and despite my attempts to stay focused, thoughts flowed through me almost with a will of their own.

I had not eaten in over 24 hours. I looked at my fingers frozen to the rock and a morbid thought flitted through my mind. They were frozen and dead anyway. If I nibbled off the tips, it would not hurt – they had long ago gone numb. My sick sense of humour kicked in again, and I told myself that I'd had worse meals at the fire hall. I laughed to myself. This would be a story to tell the guys when I got back.

Thoughts of those meals took me to my friends at the fire hall back home. I tried to imagine what they were doing right at that moment. Were they out on a call or were they gathered in the kitchen preparing dinner? I thought about the amazing career I had built and all the rescues I had experienced with those guys.

Firefighters who work together always form a kind of comradery, maybe because the job is such a dangerous and, at times, traumatic one. I would willingly die for anyone in my department, and I knew they would do the same for me. I thought about the crazy things we had done together, the lives we had saved. Then I thought about the lighter moments at the hall when we were waiting for the next call to come in.

Pranks are a part of life at a fire hall. Because the job is so stressful, I think we all feel the need to let off steam. My colleagues at the fire hall had pulled a couple of good pranks on me just before the Logan trip. As I did before every expedition, I prepared for Logan by dehydrating food for the trip. The dehydrator was noisy and sometimes smelly, so I left it at the fire hall while it ran through the dehydration cycle. When cooking on the mountain I discovered that one of my fellow firefighters had put his dirty sock in the dehydrator with the food. That meal consisted of food and a dirty sock. Mike Danks (also a firefighter) declared it was delicious! Another meal had been liberally seasoned with hot sauce – enough that tears were streaming down our faces as we ate it. Still, I would have killed for either of those meals as I clung to the rock on the col.

I am not sure if I really would have resorted to cannibalism. I could not let go of the rock anyway so it was a moot point. My fingers were firmly frozen in place. Crazy thoughts go through your head when you are starving and dying of thirst.

"You are an idiot," I told myself over and over. I felt immensely stupid. Anger flared to life inside me. I was so highly trained. I knew the cardinal rule about attaching every thing to your person; if it is not attached to you, it is gone. And still I had taken off the gloves and mitts without bothering to attach them to anything. How could I have overlooked them?

I kept going over it in my mind. It was only going to take 20 to 30 seconds to light the stove, but still, I knew better. I could blame exhaustion or dehydration, but I did not believe it. I just kept asking myself, "How could you get into this situation? You're smarter than this, Erik. You know better than this. This should not be happening." I started to hope that this was a terrible nightmare that I would soon wake up from. But deep down I knew it wasn't a nightmare. This was real.

As soon as the storm hit and my hand started to fail, I had realized the risk I'd taken in lending Linda that fleece mitt. I could only blame overconfidence for that mistake. When you climb you have to look out for yourself first. You don't offer your gear to someone else unless it is absolutely essential. Linda did not have to summit Logan. I could have ignored her desire to summit and continued down the mountain with my fleece mitts. Still, I did want her and Gord to have the best shot at summiting. I always wanted to be the good guy – the hero. I kicked myself. Maybe I should have told Linda I did not have a mitt to spare. Lending a hand has gotten me into trouble before and more than likely will get me in trouble again.

That said, I had to admit that the fleece mitt would not likely have made any difference to my hands. Even with the four layers of gloves I had left, the fingers on my left hand had begun to trouble me as soon as the storm hit; and my fully protected right hand was feeling the pain shortly after. With the extreme temperatures on Logan, I highly doubted that having both fleece layers would have helped much, and they would have blown away anyway as I would have removed them in my attempt to light the stove.

It didn't matter now. Unless there was a miracle, my hands were in serious jeopardy now.

I wondered what I could have done differently. I went over it again in my mind. We'd checked the weather reports. We even called Tim Jones by satellite phone to double-check the forecast. The reports were favourable. As the storm continued to blast my body, I wondered how conditions could have changed so radically.

I later found out that conditions like that rarely do change so radically on Logan. While it is prone to freak storms, the one we found ourselves in was an extratropical cyclone; we were in arctic hurricane-like conditions. The kind of storm we were experiencing does not develop often in the kinds of conditions that were predicted for that day. In fact, the chances of an extratropical storm to have developed were about 1 per cent. Call it bad luck, or call it fate.

As I continued to grip the rock, the pain in my hands began to take over, becoming the focus of my attention. Excruciating, indescribable pain. The pain moved up my fingers and into my hands, over my wrists, inching toward my elbows; as it moved, it left nothing but numbness behind. While the pain was constant, it was always moving, and as it moved, it seemed to take the part of my body it had just ravaged with it.

Paralysis started to set in. I could not move my fingers. An hour after lodging myself under the rock, I could not move my wrist. I recognized that the extremities of my body were freezing, that the damage would be irreparable.

The worse part was that there was nothing I could do. My hands would feel so cold, and then they would feel as if they were burning. Suddenly, it felt as if I were holding a hot iron. My automatic reaction was to let go, but I could not let go because the burning was not coming from anything I could get away from. It was coming from my own body.

In the conditions we found ourselves, wearing the gear we were wearing, frostbite starts to develop in an estimated five minutes. Frostbite actually occurs as part of a biological survival strategy. Your body automatically conserves heat by restricting blood flow to your skin and outer extremities. Eventually, the flow of blood to the affected area stops, which means ice crystals form, and the cells in the area begin to die. This was happening to all my fingers and both my hands.

They say God only gives you what you can bear and maybe that is the case, but I think that realization comes after you undergo a bad experience. I kept thinking, "I cannot take this, I cannot take this. I can't do it." But there was no escape. I didn't think I could stand the pain any longer, but I couldn't escape it either. There was no way for me to get away from it.

I tried to focus on other things. I told myself that I was lucky to be in the wilderness instead of stuck behind some desk in the city. For as long as I could remember I loved to be out in the mountains. My parents say I started climbing when I was about nine months old. I would climb out of my crib and toddle around the house. It got so bad, my dad took to putting a piece of plywood over my crib to keep me in at night.

When I was about four years old, I went out in my backyard and decided to climb a tree. I just looked up and started to climb. I climbed right to the top of the 15-metre (50-ft) tree. That was my first experience with learning that getting to the top is only half of the climb. My dad heard my yells from inside the house. When he came out into the yard he couldn't find me, until he looked up. I don't think my dad enjoyed climbing that tree as much as I did.

I spent time in the wilderness on my own from a young age. As a teenager, I would head up the mountain behind my home with my sleeping bag and tent, and sleep outside overnight. "I love extreme conditions," I reminded myself.

But memories of the North Shore Mountains were ripped from my mind as the pain in my hands demanded my full attention. I knew exactly what was happening. And I knew what to expect.

Terror began to fill me as I thought about my hands. It wasn't just the pain. I could put up with the pain – I couldn't escape it anyway. It hurt. It was the most painful thing in my life. But like all pain, it goes away eventually.

But my thoughts plagued me. I was thinking of the tips of my fingers. They did not hurt at all anymore. There was no pain there. I knew that meant they were dead.

Then I started to realize the numbness was moving. I thought, "Oh, my God, I can't feel my wrist." And the whole time I was calculating, "Okay, well, if I got saved now I'd probably get cut here so I'd be able to get those prosthetic claw things." I was terrified of the idea of those prosthetic arms because I knew if I ended up with those, my career, and life as I knew it, would be over.

First I was worried about my fingertips. Then I was worried about my hands, then my arms. By the time I froze to my elbow I didn't care about the pain or the prospect of prosthetic arms anymore. I just really wanted to live.

As I lay huddled behind and beneath the rock, realizing that I was losing my hands and probably a good part of my arms, despair settled over me like I'd never experienced before in my life. I had enough. I wanted the pain to stop. I wanted to live, but I also thought of how easy it would be to give up. All I had to do was unzip my jacket and I would die. It would be so quick; it would be over in about ten minutes. My hands were frozen to about mid-forearm by that stage, my buddies had been gone for several hours, and I was desolate.

I overcame these thoughts, though. I erased them and instead entered into what I can only now describe as an intense survival mode. I made a conscious, unwavering decision to live. I told myself: "I'm not choosing death. I'm going to choose life!"

Ales Ponec and Gord Ferguson discuss the route. PHOTO BY ISABEL BUDKE

An easy day of acclimatization for Barry Mason, Ales Ponec and Gord Ferguson. PHOTO BY ISABEL BUDKE

The NSR team indulges in a well-deserved rest at camp. PHOTO BY ALES PONEC

On my first trip to Nepal with a side trip to Tengboche Monastery.

Cooking up a storm. PHOTO BY ISABEL BUDKE

As close as it gets to being dark on Mount Logan in May. PHOTO BY ISABEL BUDKE

Mike Danks with the untouched valley behind him. PHOTO BY MIKE DANKS

Gord Ferguson and Don Jardine ponder the route. PHOTO BY ISABEL BUDKE

Erik Bjarnason and Alex Snigurowicz resting up for the next day's climb. PHOTO BY MIKE DANKS

Building the camp. PHOTO BY ISABEL BUDKE

Erik with supplies galore. PHOTO BY ISABEL BUDKE

A serac on the cusp of wiping out the trail. PHOTO BY MIKE DANKS

A well-groomed trail up to the next camp. PHOTO BY MIKE DANKS

Setting up the monster camp. PHOTO BY ISABEL BUDKE

Erik Bjarnason and Barry Mason on the trail. PHOTO BY ISABEL BUDKE

Just your average day. PHOTO BY ISABEL BUDKE

Erik on the West Peak summit bid. PHOTO BY ISABEL BUDKE

Weather is always a concern on Logan. PHOTO BY ISABEL BUDKE

Barry Mason and Isabel Budke attempt to get aid for trapped climbers. PHOTO BY ISABEL BUDKE

126

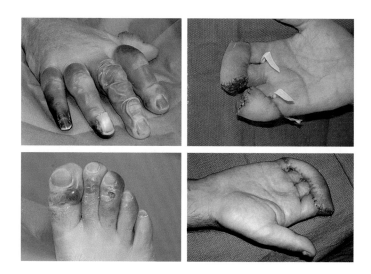

Above, left: The aftermath of frost bite. Bottom: Erik's feet also took a beating, but they survived intact.

Above, right: Skin flap over viable bone. The first of many operations in July 2005. Bottom: skin flap over viable bone.

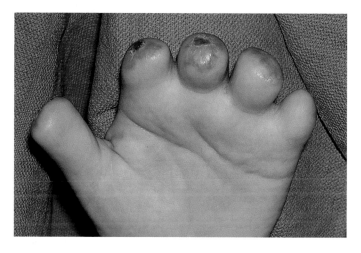

Erik's hands after reconstruction.

Retelling my story of survival at the Vancouver General Hospital Burn Ward with Mike Danks and Don Jardine.

Erik returns to the job he loves. PHOTO BY KELSEY TOEVS

10   "Will You Remember Me?"

*"Probably no other sport creates such a feeling
of oneness with Mother Nature. Attached to a
mountainside by fingertips and toes, the climber
necessarily becomes part of the rock – or else."*

—BOB MADGIC

May 26, 2005 – Prospector Col

As I huddled behind the rock, I was always calculating how
much longer I thought Alex and Don would be before they
would come back from building the snow cave. As time
dragged on, I started getting more and more worried.

Normally it would only take a couple of hours to build a
good snow cave. Building a snow cave can actually be fun if
you're not building one in order to survive. I used to make
them with my children. We would go to the mountains to
build them, and my kids would sleep in them. I smiled at
the memory, remembering how comfortable those little
caves used to be. Our body heat would warm them up to

about 0°C, so the outermost layer of snow on the interior walls melted but then turned into a layer of hard ice because of the cold snow behind it; it was like being in a little house. There were no windows but it was comfortable. The kids loved it.

As those memories ran through my mind and the winds continued buffeting my body, I started to imagine Don and Alex making a cozy little snow cave. I kept telling myself that all I had to do was live until they came back to get me. "Just a few more hours, Erik, and this will be over," I kept telling myself. Then they would come and get me and throw me into the nice little cave they were building. Once in the cave I figured it would warm up to zero, and maybe we would have a chance to live.

The thought of that little, 0°C cave seemed like heaven because I was now in -56°C (-68°F) with the wind chill. It was a cold I had never experienced before in my life. It was a cold I never could have imagined. But I kept thinking that if I could hold on for just a little bit longer I would be with my friends. And I had a strong overriding feeling that once we were together again we would be okay.

To help pass the loneliness and time, I listened to the music coming through my headphones. As soon as I'd found shelter behind the boulder, I'd dug the headphones out and put them on. I was listening to Canadian singer/songwriter Sarah McLachlan. As I held onto the rock, I closed my eyes and heard Sarah's voice, and tried to allow a deep calmness to sweep over me. The lyrics "I will remember you. Will you remember me?" floated through my head, and my thoughts shifted toward my own death and how it would affect the people in my life. I couldn't help thinking this, even though I had chosen to live.

I hoped people would remember me. I hoped my kids would remember me. I knew my parents would remember me. I knew that the odds were against us getting off the mountain. The music was incredibly sad, but at the same time it was incredibly peaceful.

Just as I would slip into a state of real calmness and start to relax a bit, a gust of wind would rip one ear bud out of my ear and the wind would fill my head. I was jerked from the temporary respite I'd found back into the horror of my current reality. I was brutally reminded that I was at the mercy of the mountain and the storm.

After these ear-bud-ripping blasts, I would slowly work the headphone back into my ear, using my shoulder to stuff it in. After a long time, the music would block out the storm, and it would be calm again for a time. I closed my eyes and floated away on the music. And then wind would rip the music from me again. And the process would start all over again.

Too soon, my batteries died and the slight respite I had found was lost.

After that happened, time really started to drag on, and despair filled me like never before. I felt as if I were the only living thing on this horror of a mountain. And loneliness engulfed me. I did not want to die by myself. I wanted my friends. I desperately did not want to die alone. I missed Alex and Don, even if the conditions were too bad to do much more than huddle together. I desperately wanted someone with me if I was going to die. I wanted at least one witness to be there. Someone to say they had seen what had happened to me; someone who would look into my eyes as I was dying and tell me it was okay.

I knew I was in bad shape. I was starting to become hypothermic. I didn't think I could hold on much longer. The longer I was on my own, the more I realized that death was becoming a very real possibility.

I didn't think that I could survive much longer. My hands freezing to the rock was what had saved me from being blown off the mountain, but nothing was protecting me from the harsh temperatures. I didn't think the window for survival out in the open like this could be very long.

I started to wonder where Don and Alex were. I had calculated that it would only take two or three hours for them to make the snow cave and then they would come back for me. Two hours, maximum. Three hours, I told myself, if the cave was going to be really nice.

Three hours had already passed. Because my mitts were gone, I could see my watch on my wrist so I was only too aware of the passage of time.

I began checking my watch more and more frequently. But the more often I checked, the slower time seemed to a crawl. I would check my watch after what I thought was half an hour only to find that just a few minutes had slipped by. I challenged myself to not look at my watch for at least an hour. So I waited and waited. The pain infused my mind. I couldn't escape it. Finally, I just couldn't stand it anymore, and I looked my watch again hoping that an hour or more had passed. I stared at it in disbelief. Ten minutes. Only ten minutes had gone by. Time had become its own torture.

As close to six hours crawled past, I became convinced that something bad had happened to my friends. I wore my radio against my skin because keeping it warm, close to my body, would help preserve the batteries. I started to focus on trying to figure out a way to press the transmission button without my hands. After some manoeuvring and a lot of false starts, I finally was able to devise a way to squeeze my arms together and send a transmission.

Overcome with relief, I started calling to Alex and Don. "Alex, Don, what's taking so long?"

I waited a few minutes, but there was no reply. "Don, Alex, it's Erik. I don't know how much longer I can last."

Still there was no reply. Despair swept over me again, obliterating the momentary hope I'd felt when I figured out how to send the transmission. I knew that even if they were making the most deluxe snow cave it would not take any more than three hours, and now they had been gone almost double that time. And they wouldn't just ignore my calls. Something had definitely happened to them.

As trained rescue workers, Don and Alex would be particularly aware of the time passing. They would know that I couldn't last too long wrapped in a sleeping bag out in the open. They didn't even know I had found the rock for shelter.

A feeling that they were gone filled me. I was suddenly very certain that I was alone on the mountain. Fear for my friends blocked out my pain. Could Don and Alex be dead?

I choked back a sob. Anger filled me. This wasn't fair. How could this happen to us? We were trained professionals; we knew how to survive in these conditions. We also were completely prepared. Over and over again I kept trying to think of what we could have done differently. But I came up with no satisfying answers. It seemed to me that bad luck had been dogging us since we left our tent the previous morning.

My mind started to come up with a variety of scenarios as to what had happened to Alex and Don. What if one or both of them had been blown off the mountain? Or if they had simply collapsed due to the cold? I refused to believe that they would just give up on me. I knew that even if, after six hours, they assumed I was dead, they would come back and check before writing me off.

Holding onto hope, I tried again and again. "Don, Alex, how much longer are you going to be?"

All that came back in return was the howling of the wind and the static of my radio. The loneliness was overpowering. But refusing to give up easily, I waited a few minutes and then I called again. Then again. I did this for more than 30 minutes.

Finally, the last threads of hope slipped away with the wind. Convinced that my friends were not coming back for me, I started to think of what else I could do. I needed to have a back-up plan.

Don had told me they would try to come back. I knew they would try if they could, but after all the time that had passed with no contact I had to face reality and accept the fact that they were gone. Either they had not survived the storm themselves or, for some reason, they could not come back.

It was now obvious that I was on my own. And if I

didn't do something to help myself, I was going to die alone. The thought terrified me. I could not just lie there and die. I had to try something. Anything.

I transmitted another message. This time I said, "I cannot do this anymore." I did not know if anyone could hear me, but I could not just lie there waiting for death to claim me.

My survival instinct had kicked in once again. What options did I have for getting off the mountain? There must be something I could do, something I had not thought of.

Then I started focusing on the camp below me. I wondered if there was a shortcut to getting down. Could I go off the front face of the col and drop down below?

I thought about it for a few minutes. The drop off was not extreme. I was on the col, but I thought the decline to the camp below us was gradual. Normally we would never take the route I was considering down the mountain. The safe route was behind the mountain and up the back. But my options were seriously limited. I could not walk without my crampons on, and I had lost them with the tent anyway. My hands were utterly useless. There was really no other option, as far as I could see. If I let go of the rock and rolled down the col toward where Barry and Isabel were, I thought I might have a chance.

Of course finding the camp in the midst of the storm would be a challenge even if I did survive the fall off the cliff. But I thought I could blow a whistle every half-hour or so and try to find camp. Barry could not come up and get me because if he tried he would find himself in just as much trouble as I was in. In addition to that, we'd lost radio contact with him so he had no idea what was happening up on the col. I figured he either assumed we were dead or that we were sitting out the storm in our tent.

I knew that the snow accumulation lower on the mountain would be even more than what I was facing up on the col. Most of the snow that was falling near me was being blown away by the high winds. Even if Barry knew I was coming, I couldn't expect him or Isabel to leave safety to look for me. To do so would mean that they might never be able to find their camp again. The only thing they could possibly do was tie a rope around themselves and then go out as far as the length of the rope, over and over again in different directions. But that would be risking frostbite. It would be crazy. No, I told myself, I was truly on my own.

I couldn't stay where I was. I refused to just lie there and die. I decided I was just going to roll down the front face of the mountain, land down on the flat and hope I would not be so broken up that I would not be able to walk. If I could walk, I would start blowing sharply into my whistle.

I squeezed my arms together and activated my radio again, relaying my plans to whoever might be listening. "I can't stay here anymore. I'm going to roll down the front face of the col. I think I have a decent chance of making it. Once I get down there, I'll try to find camp. I have my whistle and I'll do blasts. Listen for me."

I was contemplating how I would get my hands off the rock, as they were frozen solid, when a familiar voice bellowed in my ear. It was Don. He said, "No, no! Stay where you are, Erik! We're coming for you."

|| Snow Grave

"The greatest skill I ever had, though,
was the one I started with: being able to suffer
for long periods of time and not die."

— BREE LOEWEN

May 26, 2005 – Prospector Col

Relief and joy flooded through me. My friends were alive. I wouldn't have to enact my desperate plan. They were coming for me.

As I waited for them, I vaguely wondered why had they not answered any of my radio messages, especially as I had become more and more desperate. I found out later that they had lost contact with me as soon as they disappeared down the other side of the col. Searching for a bit of respite from the storm, they had dug the snow cave on the north side of the col, where it was slightly less exposed than where we had pitched our tent. But with line-of-sight radios, it wasn't until they started back for me that the radio kicked in and we had contact.

The silence on Don's and Alex's part also reflected the problems they, themselves, were facing. For a very long time, they had nothing to tell me. They were having their own troubles building the snow cave.

Logan is the second-highest mountain in North America and it is known for its severe storms and powerful winds. In fact, the winds are so powerful that despite the amount of snow that had fallen in the storm, there was almost no snow on the ground in the col area. Most of it had been blown away by the 108-km/h (67-mph) winds. All that was left was bluish-coloured ice, like the kind that made up the glaciers below us.

To make matters worse, our snow shovels had been lost with the rest of our gear when the tent had blown off the col. The only tools Don and Alex had to build the snow cave with were an ice axe and a pot lid. So they used the ice axe to chip away at the ice and then the pot lid to scrape the ice out of the snow cave. It was gruelling work in the freezing cold temperatures.

In those conditions, what would normally have taken only an hour or two, in a different climate with proper gear, took them six hours to build.

Happiness flooded me when they arrived. For a moment my joy overrode my despair. But I was soon reminded of the awful truth: my hands were gone. As Don tried to get me to move, I found that I could not physically let go of the rock.

"Erik! Come on, we have to go!" Alex yelled at me, not realizing why I wasn't following him.

138

"I can't!" I shouted back.

"You have to," Don said. "We can't be out here much longer."

I realized that they thought I was refusing to let go of the rock. They didn't know that I was stuck to it. "No, I *can't* let go!" I shouted.

Don looked confused, then stepped closer and saw my hands. They were completely frozen to the rock. His expression was grim.

The winds were gusting just as strongly as they had been when our tent blew away. We needed to get out of the wind before it blew us off the mountain. Don tugged on my arms, but my hands were frozen fast to the rock.

Finally, Don knelt on my hands and that broke the frozen grip of my fingers on the rock. I stood for the first time in six hours, my knees aching and stiff. Dizziness washed over me, and I thought I'd black out, but then I straightened as much as I could in the storm. Shakily, I followed them through the blizzard, my focus on Alex's back.

I was shocked when they came to a stop only a few minutes later. All that time, they had only been about 15 metres (50 ft) away from me. The storm was so strong and visibility was so poor that I could not hear or see them. They could have been 16 kilometres (10 mi) away instead of 15 metres.

When I saw the hole in the ground that marked the entrance to the cave, I was disappointed. My dreams of a cozy little snow house were immediately doused. It was more like a sardine can than a cave. Then a dark thought came into my head, "Oh, my God. It's like a grave. That's how they're going to find us when the storm is over. We're going to be dead, frozen, three deep in the ground."

The injustice of it all hit me. Every time I would get a glimmer of hope, something would happen to quash it.

But I had to focus on the positive. We now had some shelter. It was better than being completely exposed as I had been for the last six hours or so. All we had left of our gear from the tent was one insulated sleeping pad and two sleeping bags. Those items had fallen out of the tent with me before it disappeared into oblivion.

We put the sleeping pad on the very bottom of the 1-metre (3-ft) deep impression to provide some insulation from the icy, snow-packed floor of the cave. Then we put one of the sleeping bags on top of it. I crawled in first, then Alex squeezed in on his side beside me and Don climbed in last. I stifled a laugh as a ridiculous thought flitted through my mind: we were like a triple-decker sandwich.

Don's feet were still sticking out of the opening. None of us had been able to dry our feet out the night before, and I thought his feet must have been wet from sweat and snow. With them sticking out, they were at extremely high risk for frostbite. So we gave Don the other sleeping bag. The plan was for him to wrap the sleeping bag around his feet; this way, the sleeping bag would also cover the opening and help keep all the heat in the cave. We hoped the temperature in the cave would rise to 0°C in about an hour.

Don got the sleeping bag wrapped snugly around his feet with no problem, but when he went to lie back, another brutal gust of wind whipped up and actually sucked the sleeping bag right out of the opening. It was like someone standing outside had pulled the bag out.

It took us all a moment to process what had just happened. We lay there and just looked at one another in disbelief. Then all at once we started to laugh. It was either laugh or cry. And I figured none of us wanted to cry because then our eyelids would be frozen open.

We sobered up pretty quickly. Now we were stuck with nothing covering the entrance to the cave. Most of our body heat was escaping, while spindrift just kept coming in, making sure we didn't warm up too much. For a long, long time we lay there like that. Soon I felt myself drifting away, and I lost all track of time and space.

As we lay there, three deep in our communal grave, I became convinced that we were going to die. I just wondered how long it would take. And I wondered which one of us would go first. Don must have felt the same way. He wrote a goodbye message to his wife and tucked it in his jacket. I guess he figured that if they found our bodies, they'd find the note and give it to her.

Alex was so optimistic though. It was almost annoying. He kept saying that it would just be a matter of time before we were found. I didn't want to remind him that no one was looking for us. He talked about what he would do when he got home. But as the hours passed, his optimistic talk started to make less and less sense. I could tell he was starting to suffer from serious hypothermia.

As I was drifting off on a sea of pain and fatigue, I suddenly heard Alex's voice, the anger in his tone strong. "Don, get me a Pepsi."

Don told him to settle down, but Alex was irate, accusing Don of withholding the imaginary beverage on purpose.

"Alex, there's no Pepsi, man," I told him wearily, hoping to break into the hypothermia-induced hallucination that he seemed to be trapped in.

After grumbling for a while, he fell silent. I thought he might have passed out or maybe I did. I wasn't sure.

I was in so much pain; I was consumed by it. Conversation disappeared and I hovered on the brink of consciousness. When I was able to concentrate on something else besides the pain, I focused on the fact that both Don and Alex were in a bad way. I could tell they were becoming more and more hypothermic and, at the same time, I thought that except for my hands, I was just fine. When we reflected on this later, it seemed that we all had the same perception. Each one of us thought that the other two were going hypothermic, but each of us thought himself to be fine. In reality, at this stage, all of us were suffering from severe hypothermia.

As I lay there and time clicked by I would have periods of despair interspersed with memories of comical moments. I told myself that if I had to die, this was probably as a good a time as any. I had racked up my credit card bill to go on this climb and done a prank at the fire hall before I left.

Thoughts of the fire hall made me smile. I distracted myself by imagining what was happening back at work. Before I left for Logan I had made a stink bomb out of some cream and some old moose meat I had found in the fridge. I put it in a plastic container and hid it under the bunks in the fire-hall dorm room. I figured it had probably blown up by now. I was sure the guys would know exactly who had planted it there.

But then I started worrying that they would think it was a HazMat terrorist attack or something weird, and I would be in serious trouble. I told myself, it might be better to die on the mountain than to go back to that.

Thoughts flitted through my mind one after another, and soon they were blending together. Sometimes they made sense and sometimes they didn't. My emotions were changing by the minute. All at once I was filled with immense gratitude and I thought about what a fantastic life I'd had with all my trips and all the great experiences. Joy so pure it brought tears to my eyes. And I felt contentment and peace wash over me. But then I thought about my children and what it would do to them when they heard I had died on the mountain. I was going to leave them without a father growing up. It hurt too much to dwell on for long.

Then I thought about my daughter, Joline, and I wondered what would happen to her. I wondered if she would be glad or sad that I was dead. Or maybe she would not care.

I could not shut my mind off. I was so cold and so uncomfortable; it was impossible to sleep. And with hypothermia setting in, the last thing I wanted to do was to fall asleep for fear I would never wake up. Soon I knew I would start to hallucinate like Alex had because I had been awake for a couple of days at this point with no food, no water and I was at the end of what the body can take. I knew that eventually my body was going to shut down, and it would start with my brain. It seemed certain to me that our snow grave would be the place where the three of us would die.

Hypothermia occurs when your core temperature drops below 35°C (95°F). At first you experience minor symptoms like shivering, but as it progresses you start to feel sluggish and your movements become slow and laboured. In addition, you start to feel mildly confused even though you may appear alert. As it progresses further, you start to experience amnesia and have difficulty speaking and your mind does not work right. Looking back, it is clear to me that our cognitive processes were affected on some level.

At one point, Don had to get out of the confined space. The sardine can we were in was driving him mad. He climbed out and wandered around in the storm. Finally, Alex, who all of a sudden seemed to be just fine again, went and got him and brought him back.

We huddled in the cave, exhausted. My mouth was so dry it was an effort to say anything. I couldn't swallow. And the wind continued to howl so loudly that even if I felt like talking, I didn't have the strength to yell above the ongoing roar.

Despite the sleeping bag flying away, the snow cave was warmer than it had been out in the storm. My hands started to warm up, and feeling returned to parts of them. I remembered being a kid and playing out in the cold. My hands would get so cold it would hurt, but then when I would come inside the house where it was warm, they would hurt more. It was the same now except in the extreme. As the feeling returned it brought with it a pain so searing that I wanted to die.

But I reminded myself that if I could feel pain then maybe my hands weren't as bad off as I thought they were. Maybe there was a chance they could be saved. And as those thoughts flitted through my mind, I started to crave the pain.

Unfortunately, for my hands to be saved, we would have to be rescued. I didn't think that seemed possible. Alex was unconscious again and Don was quiet. I started to calculate how much longer we could last. No food, no water and frigid temperatures. I figured if we were lucky we could maybe survive another hour or two. Three at the most.

As that negative thought invaded my mind, I started to notice something else. The noise outside was starting to dissipate. I held my breath, not daring to believe what I was hearing. But it was true. As quickly as the storm had come, it disappeared.

12 Radio Free Logan

> *"Mountains are not fair or unfair,*
> *they are just dangerous."*
>
> —REINHOLD MESSNER

May 27, 2005 – Prospector Col

"Don!" I croaked. "Is it over?"

Don looked at me and then sat up. Quickly he crawled out of the cave. Alex and I followed.

As we emerged, we saw blue skies and sunshine. At first I thought maybe all of us were hallucinating, but it was real. After 36 hours of enduring the relentless blizzard we were now in fair weather.

I looked around in disbelief. The clouds had parted and the wind subsided. It went from −56°C (−68°F) with wind chill to −25°C (−13°F) in what seemed like 15 minutes.

I studied the sky, dumbfounded. The storm had definitely broken, but I could still see it. I wondered if we were just in the centre of it. There were blue skies above us but all around us there were clouds. My heart sank as I saw that this might be only be a short reprieve, one that might not be long enough for any rescue mission to be launched. We were still in trouble, but I reminded myself that it was better than it had been. The gusting wind had slowed down for the moment.

Although the temperature was still well below 0°C, it was so much warmer than it had been during the storm that it felt like stepping into a sauna. It was also so bright that it was dazzling.

During the storm, it had been so dark I could not see anything, and then all of a sudden for a brief moment it felt like an oasis. I sat with Alex and Don on the edge of the snow cave and relief poured through me. I felt almost as if we were in a heat wave.

Not long after we crawled out of the snow cave, the radio suddenly crackled to life. It was Barry. I answered immediately.

"Hey, it's Erik. We're alive," I told him.

I could tell Barry was shocked to hear from me. After losing radio contact with us for hours, and our last conversations revolving around farewell messages for our loved ones, he had feared the worst. Both Barry and Isabel had assumed that we had died overnight in the storm. It was almost unthinkable that anyone could survive those conditions, especially without supplies or shelter.

Barry and Isabel were relieved we were alive, but I told them the stark truth – I didn't know how long we would be. There was no question that we were in bad shape. Alex had lost consciousness again, and I thought he must be close to death. Don was sitting a short distance from me on some rocks, his expression blank. My hands were excruciatingly painful, and I was afraid of what I would see if I took my gloves off.

Barry told me he and Isabel would rope together and start up the mountain to our position. I knew it was about a three- to four-hour climb in good weather. I didn't want to consider how long it would take them to break trail through the remnants of the storm.

I told him we would wait to hear from them, knowing it could be many hours before they would arrive. A little voice in my head asked if I really thought it was possible for them to get to us through the deep snow, but I pushed the voice aside.

Two hours after I'd spoken to Barry, I was getting increasingly worried about Alex. He hadn't gained consciousness since Barry and I had talked, and I was starting to wonder if he was even alive anymore. My hands were too painful for me to attempt to undo his gear and see if he was breathing. I couldn't discern any rise or fall of his chest.

"Barry, it's Erik."

The radio was silent. I tried again. And again. There was no reply from Barry on the radio. After 20 minutes or so, I realized that we were once again on our own.

Over 1 metre (3 ft) of fresh snow had fallen lower on the mountain. I knew that in order for Barry and Isabel to get to us they would have to come up an avalanche chute. The rescue route was extremely dangerous because there was all this new snow on top of solid ice. The risks to any rescue team would be high.

I later found out that just as they promised us, Barry and Isabel did set out to try to help us as soon as the storm broke. As honourable team members and professionally trained rescue members, they couldn't turn their backs on us; it was their job to rescue people. So they roped together and started out. They spent about an hour trying to make progress, but they only went about 500 metres (1,600 ft).

At that stage they realized that it was foolhardy to try to reach us on foot. It would take four or five days for them to get to us at the rate they were moving. They turned around and retreated. They decided not to tell us that they were aborting the rescue attempt because they were worried we would give up all hope if we knew. Instead they decided to try to find help farther down the mountain.

Barry and Isabel made the right decision. There is no doubt in my mind that they would have died trying to get to us. As it turned out, if they had not retreated, we all would very likely have perished on the mountain. But because I still thought they were coming for us, I decided to stay and see what happened. Alex wasn't in any shape to move anyway. Don was quiet, sitting in the sun. I knew his feet must be aching as much as my hands were, since they had been exposed to the storm for most of the night.

As I sat there, my thoughts drifted to Linda Bily and Gord Ferguson on the Plateau. I had no idea what had happened to them. The last time I had seen them, they were going for their summit attempt, and then the storm blew in. I knew that they could be in as much trouble as we were, if not worse. A little part of me still somehow knew they were safe and that they would soon be heading down the mountain. They would find us.

Even though we were out of the snow cave and we were alive for the moment, I felt like a zombie. I could not talk, and I really could not make much sense of what was happening. I was so disoriented from hypothermia that all I could do was sit on the lip of our shelter.

By now I knew that Alex was unconscious, not dead. He had started groaning and mumbling. But it was pretty obvious that if he did not get help fast, he was going to die despite his optimistic predictions of the night before that we would make it off the mountain alive.

I had him in my lap, cradling him. Don wasn't talking, but he looked like he was doing pretty well, all things considered. I thought he was in best shape of the three of us. He had a sudden spark of energy and got on the radio and started calling for help again. But his rational calls for help would dissolve into hypothermic talk. He kept asking when the helicopters would arrive as if it had already been organized that rescue helicopters were on their way. I was just too spent to do anything.

Don focused on contacting Linda and Gord above us. I think he was hoping they would be able to come down and assist us until the lower team could get to us. But the rock band between us meant that no transmission was getting through. After about 30 minutes of trying to get in touch with them, I saw his shoulders slump and he gave up in defeat. He sat back down on the rock and stared off into the distance, his face stony with disappointment.

151

I felt the same sense of despair. Incredibly, we had survived the storm but now the only people who knew we were in trouble couldn't get to us quickly and no one else had any idea about the predicament we were in.

I shook my head, wondering why we had survived the storm, only to die anyway. I closed my eyes as the reality of our situation once again crashed down on me.

Suddenly the silence of the mountain was broken by a jovial voice.

"Radio Free Logan is back on the air," Gord Ferguson's joking voice fractured the morning air.

I stared at my radio in disbelief, wondering if I was hallucinating. It only took me a minute to realize that I wasn't. I squeeze my arms together to send out a transmission. My old friend Gordie was about to get the surprise of his life.

13   Help!

> *"Only those who will risk going too far*
> *can possibly find out how far they can go."*
>
> —T.S. ELIOT

May 27, 2005 – Prospector Col

Unbeknownst to us, Linda and Gord had abandoned their summit attempt fairly early on due to high winds and had made it safely back to Advance Camp. From their vantage point on the summit climb they'd had a better view of the range than we had from the Plateau.

They had seen the sky becoming more and more grey and overcast while the winds aloft increased. The storm did not hit their location at Advance Camp with the same vengeance as it had hit us because it was much lower and more sheltered than where we were, stranded on the col. But as the storm built, even their more protected area was hit hard.

Gord told us it started as a normal hoolie. The first warning signs of what was to come were the very high wind gusts, which shook the fly of their tent and deformed the tent poles more than usual. The first night was a fairly standard stormy night for them; the winds buffeted and snow accumulated, but things didn't really get going until around daybreak on Thursday (at that point we'd already been battling the storm in our tent for almost 12 hours).

By then the biggest gusts of wind came with lots of warning. Gord would later say it sounded like an approaching train. The wind would hit their tent wall, pushing it closer and closer to the floor.

Gord said he saw the tent fly peel back from the vestibule and flap wildly. He had to dive through the door to grab a corner. Together, he and Linda secured the fly, collapsing the vestibule and reinforcing the tie downs. Although they had an excellent MEC Nunatak tent, a very robust time-tested design, they soon realized that there was a real possibility that they could lose their tent, just as we had done. The tent body, poles and fly were designed to work together, and if one part failed, the whole structure would go. Without the fly, the tent body would shred.

But Linda and Gord still had all their gear on a less-exposed part of the mountain. So they tucked in for some serious digging. With a shovel and single snow saw, they set out to cut blocks, digging snow both off the tent and onto the wall, and expanding their perimeter. To block the prevailing wind and protect your camp, you need at least one wall. Sometimes you need a wall on two or three sides, but their wall extended to 360 degrees, with a moat. Building it was an all-day job done in short spurts of activity for as long as they could stay out. Needless to say, every bit of gear, in the tent and on them, was soaked by the effort. But over time their camp became safer.

When the storm finally died during the wee hours of the morning on Friday, they woke to a calm and crystal-clear dawn. Their tent had been buried and their ski tips barely broke through the new snow, but Gord thought the challenge (except for trail breaking) was over. For a laugh, he fired up the FRS radio, knowing it could not reach anyone over the ridge that rose above them.

When Gord heard my voice, he was shocked. As I explained our situation to him, I could tell he was stunned. When he didn't respond for a minute, I told him, "Gord, we're hanging by a thread."

Immediately he got to work. As a long-time NSR member, he had no trouble jumping right into rescue mode.

I knew we were in dire condition. I did not sugar coat the situation for Gord. I told him that Don was hypothermic, I had severe frostbite and Alex was going to be dead within the next hour if we did not get help. Alex was unconscious, and I honestly didn't know if he would ever wake up.

In all my years as a rescue worker, I had never seen anybody as hypothermic as Alex was by that point. I had been on the NSR team for almost 20 years, and one of the main things we do is rescue hypothermic people. Alex was so far gone I just did not think there was any way he would make it.

Gord and Linda dumped everything that was not essential (including extra food, fuel and rope), loaded one crazy-carpet boggie, and set off breaking trail across the broad expanse of the Plateau.

They also set to work calling for help on the satellite phone. We all had paid our park fees, and rescue insurance is included in those fees. Knowing this, they first called the Royal Canadian Mounted Police (RCMP) in Haines Junction, gave them our coordinates and explained the situation. They told the RCMP that they were going to try to reach us, but it would take several hours because of the distance and deep snow. What we really needed was a rescue helicopter – it seemed it would be the only way we could possibly survive – but they also knew that there was no helicopter capable of rescuing people on Logan. Still, they hoped the RCMP would be able to dispatch their message widely, just in case some form of help was available. The RCMP confirmed the lack of a helicopter, and they did not mince words. They told Gord and Linda that they did not really believe there was anything they could do for us.

This was not the news they were hoping for. If there was no rescue helicopter, and no other form of rescue, then we were as good as dead. No. They refused to accept that. Falling back on his NSR training, Gord called our NSR team leader, Tim Jones, in Vancouver.

To his immense relief, Tim told Gord that Barry, now located at Football Field Camp on the other side of the col, had already called him on a borrowed satellite phone.

After Barry and Isabel realized that they wouldn't make enough progress to reach us, they turned around and started to ski down the mountain, searching for a team that might have a satellite phone they could borrow. They did not have to ski very far before they ran into a French team, whose members generously let them use their satellite phone.

Barry first called Parks Canada. The operator told him they did not have the manpower or equipment needed to perform a high-altitude rescue on Logan. They told him we would have to self-extricate.

Barry was stunned. He replied, "To be clear, I am telling you that three of our team members are trapped on Prospector Col. They are unable to self-extricate, and without a helicopter rescue they will die. Are you are saying there is nothing you can do?"

The Parks Canada respondent replied in the affirmative.

Without knowing what to do next, Barry called 911 in Anchorage. He explained the situation to them, but they also told him that they were not able to help. Seeing that neither Parks Canada nor the local authorities were able to provide any assistance, Barry contacted Tim Jones in Vancouver.

Tim Jones had been part of the NSR team since 1987. He was also a good friend of everybody involved. If there was one person who could find a way to get us out of the situation we were in, it would be Tim. Despite the thousands of kilometres separating us, despite the fact that he was actively entrenched in a separate rescue back at home in the North Shore Mountains, if there was a way to get us help, Tim would do it. He was an extraordinary leader and a problem solver.

The rescue team is an extremely close-knit group. We climb together, we socialize together, we save lives together. We are family. To hear members of your family are close to death is devastating.

At the time, Tim Jones was leading a rescue mission on Grouse Mountain for missing American magazine publisher David Koch. Koch had taken the Skyride up the mountain and then disappeared without a trace. Sadly, his body was found a few weeks later...he had died from hypothermia.

Koch was from the U.S. and so American officials were involved with the search. Tim was just about to go on the noon television newscast to discuss the search for Koch when he got Barry's call about us. He told Barry that he would do everything he could to help us and asked Barry to stand by to give updates.

Meanwhile, I continued to talk to Gord on the radio. Alex was not improving. It must have been extremely frustrating for Gord and Linda to ponder the situation for the almost four hours it took them to bust trail from Advance Camp through the old location of Main Camp – now an uninterrupted expanse of snow – and up to Prospector Col. But when they arrived, incredibly, we were all still alive.

Gord and Linda approached us lower on the skiable section of the slope, and they called to us from below, where they started pitching their tent. Gord later described us as hypothermic, frostbitten but somewhat ambulatory. Don was physically able to walk, as coherent as he ever is, but he was in shock, with frostbite to his hands and feet. Alex was semi-conscious, later claiming to be hibernating in what he would call "survival mode." Gord swears I was normal, apart from my frostbite. I'm not sure that's entirely accurate.

"Don, let's go," I called over to where he was sitting in the sun.

Don shook his head. "I'm going to wait here for the helicopter," he stated stubbornly, a look of determination on his face. Hypothermia was muddling his thinking.

"Come on, Don, the helicopters will see us better in the tents!" Gord yelled up.

Don looked down at the tent Linda and Gord had just finished erecting.

"They have supplies," I added.

That did it. Don got up and started heading down. Amazingly, I was able to rouse Alex from his stupor and help him down to the tent.

Once we were in the tent, I collapsed. For the first time in more than 48 hours, I was sheltered from the elements. As Linda and Gord started brewing up some soup for us, I passed out beside Don and Alex, exhaustion taking its toll.

While I was unconscious, Linda and Gord made hot drinks, and because the weather looked like it was worsening, they started building a snow wall for our location. They woke me some time later. I struggled to keep my eyes open. I felt deep fatigue threatening to pull me under again. I sipped some warm Gatorade. The moment I tasted it, I knew it was the most delicious drink I had ever had in my life. I would have paid $10 million for that drink, it was so good. There was not enough, I was so thirsty, but it was something. I gave in and closed my eyes. For the moment, our situation was stable. How long the food would last and whether or not we would be able to get off the mountain safely was still uncertain. But I was too tired to think about that.

14 My Hands

"It always seems impossible until it is done."

—NELSON MANDELA

May 27, 2005 – Prospector Col

When I regained consciousness some time later, I was acutely aware of the pain in my hands. It had pulled me from a deep slumber. As I struggled to sit up, I stared dumbly at my gloves. I was terrified to remove them and see how much damage had been caused, and yet I was morbidly curious as to what I would find.

The pain was a good sign, I reminded myself. I wouldn't feel a thing if my hands were completely dead. But at the same time, I would be kidding myself if I didn't admit that some serious damage had been done.

I decided it was time to see just how bad my hands were. Clumsily, I peeled back my gloves, and what I saw made me feel sick to my stomach. My hands were pulseless, hard, cold, and as white as marble. In places the skin had split open, and you could see frozen blood. It was like looking at something that was no longer a part of me. My fingers looked like overcooked hot dogs.

I stared at my hands in shock. An idle thought floated through my numb brain: "Wow, that's not good."

Shocked, Gord and Linda drew in their breath. Everyone around me averted their eyes, but I couldn't stop staring at my hands. Despair settled in the tent. We were warming up, but no one was optimistic. I don't think any of us really believed that help was coming. My hands were a visible reminder of how dire the situation was.

Panic started to well up inside me.

"If I do live my life is over," I thought. "What am I going to do? I can't be a firefighter; I can't be a search and rescue member. I will never climb again. I'm going to have these two stumps. I'm going to be a drain to my family. I'm going to be an invalid."

I began to hyperventilate slightly. How could you do even the simplest things without your hands? How do you wipe your own ass when you don't have hands?

A sinking sensation filled me as the full extent of my situation hit home. I had lost my fingers, hands and probably my arms. My arms were still frozen almost to my elbow. They hurt a lot, but they looked so bad. I didn't hold out much hope that they would be saved.

Even if I did live, I figured I was most likely going to be amputated at the elbows and end up with the prosthetic arms I had been thinking about during the storm. Even though I logically know a person can live a full and productive life as an amputee, the idea of losing my arms was devastating in that moment.

I struggled with the truth in a state of despair. The only two things I really excel at are mountain rescue and firefighting. With prosthetics, as strong as they make them nowadays, I did not think I would ever be able to be a firefighter again. And firefighting is my life's passion; it is not a job. It is all I have wanted to do since I was a child. The *only* thing I ever wanted to do. Heck, the only thing I probably *could* do successfully.

I looked up from my hands, my eyes slightly blurred with tears, and saw my teammates. No one tried to comfort me. No one said a word. I knew they didn't know what to say. Besides, this was not the time or place to talk about my hands or the future. We took it one moment at a time. We were all trained well enough in rescue that we knew that this was the only way forward.

As we drank more warm Gatorade, we divided up the little food Linda and Gord had with them. Even though we did not say it aloud, I started to realize that the only way for our team members to survive would be if they left me in the tent.

They had to move on if they wanted to make it, and there was no possibility of me moving on. I was not in any condition to move. I was critically injured. I could not hold anything. If they took me along, the best they could do was tie a rope to me and then to one of themselves, but if I fell on the way down, I would drag the other person over with me. I could not hold an ice axe to stop my fall. I could not even self-rescue. I would be a liability. I would not let them put themselves in such danger. Any descent would be dangerous enough without trying to carry a broken bag of bones like me down with them.

As I drank the hot Gatorade, I started to warm up. My hands started to become unbearable. A searing, knife-like pain took over. I started to focus just on my breathing to try to get through the pain. As my hands warmed, the pain was just as bad if not worse than it had been when they were freezing.

It must have been horrible for my friends to watch me going through the pain. It would have been a helpless feeling because we had no drugs, no painkillers. There was nothing they could do to stop it. I started to wish for my hands to freeze again so I would not have to feel the excruciating, overwhelming pain.

Below the obvious physical pain there was an emotional pain that I wasn't ready to deal with yet. As we sat in the tent warming up and the reality of what I had lost stared me in the face, I could not help thinking again that this might not be a bad time to die.

But the survival instinct is a strong one, and even in my despair I was starting to plan how we could get ourselves out of this situation.

With the satellite phone dead, Parks Canada unable to help us, and Barry obstructed by the snow that had fallen, as far as we knew we were on our own. But we still planned. If anyone could get out of this situation, it would be us. Five experienced outdoors people, four of us highly trained rescue workers. We started to formulate a plan for getting off the mountain alive. We were North Shore Rescue – that is what we do!

Finally, after some discussion, we came up with a tentative game plan. There were five of us now. Alex, Don and I still had our skis; they remained jammed into the snow outside where our tent had been, so we decided that two able-bodied people would escort the two injured people down to the other side of the col, where our situation would improve drastically. It was more sheltered, lower, safer, closer to our cache of food and fuel. It was also closer to rescue, and we could get ground-based support from Barry and Isabel below the col.

According to this plan, one injured person would have to be left behind. I thought it was clear that person should be me; I was so bad off at this stage that I could not even hold an ice axe. If I fell, I could not self-rescue; I could not do anything. Don's feet were frozen because they had been sticking up above the snow cave with no cover. Remarkably, once Alex warmed up, he was much better. He had some strength left, as much strength as he could have had after going through such an ordeal. At that point, he was probably the best out of the three of us so he would have the best chance of survival.

Regardless of who went down, the conditions resulting from the storm meant the descent would still be extremely dangerous. The avalanche risk was high. However, we had no other choice. In my heart I felt that no one was coming for us. They had to try to go down because if we stayed where we were, I thought we would definitely die. Reluctantly, everyone agreed. Linda and Gord would take

Alex and Don down. Then they would come back and get me.

Underneath it all we knew that the chances of anyone coming back for me were small. But none of us talked about that. The plan made sense – even though it meant I would be left, most probably to die.

Even though we all agreed to this plan, Gord said that this should be Plan B. He reasoned that we were in a stable position: we had enough food and fuel for the present, and we could safely wait. And besides, we were all too fatigued for anyone to try to move anytime soon.

With a rudimentary survival plan in place, we decided to rest for a couple of hours and then reassess the situation. In my mind, I felt they should go and leave me. I told myself it was the only way any of us would survive.

With those thoughts in my head, I drifted off to sleep. I do not know how long I had been unconscious when a massive rumbling sound pulled me from sleep. It was a loud, roaring, crashing noise that made my stomach drop and my heart race. I knew that sound from experience. I knew what it meant even as my mind told me it couldn't be true. But it was. The only thing on a mountain that makes that kind of noise is an avalanche.

15 Mobilizing the Alaska Air Guard and Jim Hood

*"You can't connect the dots looking forward;
you can only connect them looking backwards.
So you have to trust that the dots will
somehow connect in your future."*

—STEVE JOBS

May 27, 2005 – Vancouver, Alaska and Prospector Col

Back in Vancouver, Tim Jones was keeping his word and trying to think of what he could do to get us off the mountain. He still had to do his live TV broadcast at noon, which changed from a report solely on the search for the missing American, Koch, to a report that included the missing NSR members on Logan.

Tim was very close to us, and he took his job as team leader very seriously. I've seen the TV recording of that interview with him, and in it the hardened NSR leader becomes very emotional. He stated that three members of the team, three of his friends, were in a desperate, life-threatening situation on Logan.

That's how our families found out we were in trouble. Tim did not mention any names, but I think everybody had a good idea I was probably one of the members he was talking about because I always seem to get in trouble wherever I am.

After he finished the interview, Tim called my parents. My mom answered the phone and after listening to him for about two seconds became too distraught to continue. She gave the phone to my father and Tim relayed the news.

Soon, at home in Vancouver, the phones were all ringing. Everybody was trying to figure out who was missing and what was happening.

In the midst of all this, one of the American officials involved in the search for Koch said to Tim, "Well, they're up in the Yukon on Logan, that's only a couple hundred miles away from Anchorage, isn't it?"

Tim answered, "Yeah, it's a few hundred miles east of Anchorage."

And the American said, "Well, why don't you call the Alaska Air Guard?"

Tim, who obviously had no contact with the Air Guard, asked, "Do you know the number?"

Remarkably, the American official said, "Yeah, actually I do."

Tim's the only man I know who could get another country's military in the air with one phone call.

Soon the U.S. military was involved, but because we had lost contact with Barry and the satellite phone Gord had was not working properly, we had no idea this was happening and we were sticking with our own plans.

I knew that because we were trapped at 5500 metres (18,000 ft), the odds of a helicopter rescue were low. There are very few helicopters that can fly at that altitude. The Canadian Parks Service did not have access to any high-altitude helicopters. But, unknown to us, Denali National Park in Alaska did.

Jim Hood is a contract pilot stationed in Talkeetna, Alaska, who works for Evergreen Helicopters. Evergreen has an ongoing contract with parks services in Alaska, and they have an Aérospatiale SA 315B Lama helicopter, known as the "Denali Lama." The Lama was first developed in the late 1960s to meet Nepalese and Indian Air Force requirements. It was designed specifically for high-altitude flying and in 1972 set a world record that still stands today for the highest-altitude flight (climbing to 12,442 metres or 40,820 ft).

From May through to the end of July, during climbing season, Jim is on call at Denali with his Lama, and he performs numerous high-altitude rescues every year. As of that moment in 2005 he had never performed a rescue on Mount Logan (it was out of Denali's jurisdiction) but when Parks Canada coordinated with the Alaska National Guard, Denali National Park Services stepped up to help.

Jim had picked up snippets of the situation on Logan as he monitored his radio. Monitoring the radio and listening for potential rescues is part of his regular routine. If he hears that a situation is developing, he puts himself on what he calls "yellow alert."

When the call came in for Jim to prepare to join the rescue effort, he was not surprised. However, the rescue on Logan would be different than his usual missions on Denali. First, Logan is 621 kilometres (386 mi) away from Denali. Even though he had departed in his Lama as soon as he heard about the rescue, he was several hours from where we were on the mountain, and he had to stop along the way to refuel. In addition, the weather reports were mixed, indicating that the conditions on Logan were deteriorating again.

Barry was in contact with the rescue crews from Football Field, and he told them that the conditions higher up the mountain where we were located were pristine. After some convincing on his part, they started prepping for the rescue attempt. Of course, we had no idea what was happening. There was nothing we could do but huddle in the tent and try to keep warm.

Our would-be rescuers were also at the mercy of the weather. The last thing we wanted was to put anyone else in danger. As we had learned the hard way, on Logan the variability of the weather was a real concern. Help was on the way, but Mother Nature had to cooperate if we had any hope of survival.

16   Pave Hawks Overhead

> *"When I let go of what I am,*
> *I become what I might be."*
>
> —LAO TZU

May 27, 2005 – Prospector Col

The rumbling was so loud I was sure the avalanche would hit at any moment and wipe us off the mountain. But then logic filtered into my frozen, numbed brain, and I realized it could not be an avalanche; we were at the top of the col – there was nothing above us. But what was making such a noise?

Gord stuck his head out the window of the tent and looked up.

"What the hell are they doing here?" he muttered to himself.

I looked up at him blearily.

"It's a C-130 Hercules," he explained.

We spilled out of the tent with a speed that belied our poor condition. Sure enough there was the plane circling above us. As it turned and came around for another fly by, I saw the small U.S. flag on the tail of the plane. It was the U.S. military!

It seemed so random. It didn't make sense to me why the American Air Force would be there. We were so remote, and there was no reason for any planes to be anywhere around us. It seemed highly unlikely that they would be doing a training exercise so high up on Logan. Besides, we were in Canada.

I had no idea or any hope that a rescue was under way. If Gord and Linda hadn't also seen the plane, I would have assumed I was hallucinating. At this point I did not believe anyone knew we were in trouble.

And then Gord pointed and cried out, "Oh, my God, it's dipping its wings!"

I looked up, and sure enough the plane clearly dipped its wings. A spark of something I vaguely recognized as hope shot through me. I knew that when an aircraft dips its wings it is the international sign for "We see you!"

Adrenaline shot through every vein in my body as I thought, "The American military is here to help! We are saved! We're going to live!"

In the next moments the roar increased as helicopters suddenly swept down upon us. I felt as if I was in a helicopter scene out of the movie *Apocalypse Now*. All of sudden there were what seemed like five or six earth-thumping, powerful Sikorsky Pave Hawk helicopters buzzing around our tent. In reality, there were only two of them, but I was so hypothermic I didn't comprehend what I was seeing. Joy filled me. We were about to be saved! I watched as the two helicopters hovered about 15 metres (50 ft) away from us. They would hover about 3 metres (10 ft) off the ground for a minute or so and then leave and then the next one would try. But they never touched down.

As they kept doing this, I realized that they were testing the air pressure. The air pressure at 5400 metres (18,000 ft) was so low that if they landed they would not have the air pressure to power the helicopters to take off again, especially with more people on board. Jim Hood says the air is so thin at that altitude that there's not enough of it for the blades of the helicopter (even the Lama) to bite into air to give the helicopter the lift required.

High-altitude helicopter rescue is particularly dangerous work for the pilots. Landing and not having the power to be able to take off again can be catastrophic. The pilots can fly from sea level to 5500 metres (18,500 ft) in a very short period of time. Jim Hood flies the Lama with an oxygen tank but his tank only lasts 1.5 hours. If he landed and could not take off again, he could be dead or seriously incapacitated as soon as that oxygen ran out, as he would have not had time to acclimatize. It didn't take long for it to become apparent that if the Pave Hawks attempted to land, the risk was too great that they would not be able to take off again.

The knowledge crushed down on me as I slowly came to realize that the helicopters might not be able to help us. They certainly didn't seem to be landing. My hopes of climbing into a helicopter and flying off the mountain started to fade.

I deflated as I watched the Pave Hawks rise and then turn away from us. As quickly as the two helicopters had come, they were gone. Then the Hercules left as well. The silence was deafening. We were alone again. A sinking sensation started in my chest. I knew that if the U.S. military could not help us, no one could.

17   The Denali Lama

> *"I do not at all understand the mystery*
> *of grace –only that it meets us where we are*
> *and does not leave us where it found us."*
>
> —ANNE LAMOTT

May 27–28, 2005 – Prospector Col

I had been involved with many mountain helicopter rescues over the years with NSR. I knew that in certain situations a helicopter rescue with seasoned pilots could be the difference between success or failure, and in many cases, life or death. But I had never been directly involved with a high-altitude helicopter rescue. One thing was clear to me, though: the retreat of the Pave Hawks seemed to spell disaster for us.

The knowledge that there was not going to be a rescue settled over me with a bleak finality. But something miraculous was happening just as I was feeling utterly defeated. Jim Hood and his high-altitude Lama were only about a half-hour away. While I had believed that the other aircraft were abandoning us, in reality this was part of their routine in any high-altitude rescue.

Before the Lama attempts a rescue, other aircraft are sent to the scene to evaluate the terrain, location, and what kind of rescue equipment and rescue strategy might be needed. Usually these aircraft orbit the rescue site, checking every detail possible, from visibility conditions, landing spots, wind readings and temperatures, to the status of the stranded subjects.

Although I did not recognize it immediately, for the first time in three days, our luck was changing. From the time I had left the summit, anything that could go wrong had gone wrong. "Why should anything be different now?" I thought.

After the Pave Hawks disappeared, we retreated to the tent, going back to our original plan for getting off the mountain, but then we heard another helicopter approaching. Once again, Gord popped his head out of the tent and yelled at us to look.

The bubble cockpit of a helicopter came into view. From my training I knew what I was seeing: a Lama, a high-altitude helicopter. It is designed for exactly the kind of conditions we were in. It was our best chance at survival. It was certainly my only hope of survival.

I was on an emotional rollercoaster. One minute I was certain I was going to die and then the military showed up and I thought, "Oh, I'm going to live!" The next minute the military could not help, and the dire reality of our situation surfaced again. Now, with the arrival of the Lama, once again I thought, "Okay, somehow I'm going to live through this."

We rushed out of the tent, and I could see the Lama hovering about 3 metres (10 ft) off the ground in the same way the Pave Hawks had. It did this for 30 or 40 seconds and then, unbelievably, it left.

I fell to my knees. I was utterly devastated. I thought, "If this thing is designed for high altitude and it cannot help us, then nothing can." I think all of us were left with that thought as Jim flew away. It was everything I could do to keep from crying.

Although I had previously agreed to our back-up plan, I knew that plan meant fairly certain death for me. I had accepted that. But when the aircraft started arriving, hope had started to grow inside of me again. I didn't want to die. I started to believe I had a good chance at survival.

When the Lama flew away, I knew we had to go back to Plan B. And I wasn't ready to accept that anymore. In that moment, I wanted so badly to live, regardless of the damage that been done to my hands. Regardless of the type of life I might have back at home.

I sat outside the tent in the snow. It was 11 p.m. The storm had gone and the sky was still fairly light. I looked up and wondered what the point of all this was. I wondered why my hopes were being raised so high just to have them dashed again.

As I sat there, I thought about what my would-be rescuers would tell my family. Would they have to say that they'd left me on the mountain to die? Would they say there was nothing they could do to save me? I didn't envy them the task. I'd been the bearer of bad news more times than I cared to remember. I remembered one of the saddest rescues I'd been involved in. It had happened about ten years before Logan, and, tragically, it had involved a child.

Four-year-old Eagle Brown was picnicking with his family on the banks of Rubble Creek near Whistler when he disappeared. The SAR team was called out to help. Because I was the only member who had a wetsuit, before long I found myself in the frigid waters, prodding with a stick, searching for something I didn't want to find: the body of a little boy.

For three days we searched for Eagle. I prayed that by some miracle one of my teammates would find him somewhere on shore, cold and scared but safe. Deep down I knew that wasn't going to happen.

On the third day, I found Eagle in the river. He had been trapped beneath a rock in the creek. His body floated to the surface after I prodded it. I knew right away what my stick had touched was not a rock but a little boy.

As I carried Eagle to dry land, I couldn't help thinking that he looked just like a little kid. Except he didn't. The lively little guy his family had described was gone. All that remained was this small body.

I remember Eagle's parents were too distraught to identify his body. His grandfather stepped in. I remember the sense of failure that consumed me. As a rescue worker, I had wanted more than anything to be able to bring that little boy back to his family alive. But sometimes that isn't possible. Our would-be rescuers would face the same sense of failure when they told our families that we had perished on the mountain.

I sat there quietly, letting the memories and thoughts ebb away, when I heard the sound of the Lama again. About 20 minutes had passed. Jim Hood had come back!

I had no idea what he was doing. I wondered if maybe he had dumped some fuel or something so he would be lighter. At that point, I just didn't know what to expect. This time around, the Lama hovered right over the tent and a radio dropped from it.

The radio fell straight for Gord's head. He jumped out of the way at the last minute, and I laughed. It had almost beaned him right on the noggin. In the midst of all my fear and fatigue, the hilarity of the situation just swept over me. As I continued to chortle, Gord glared at me. "Very funny," he said drily as he picked up the radio.

I quickly sobered. A radio meant direct communication with our rescuers.

We got the radio, and Gord started talking to Jim Hood, who gave Gord instructions for preparing us for transport. He was there to attempt a rescue!

In the midst of his conversation with Jim, Gord kept getting an intervening radio transmission from a Yukon taxi company, telling us to get off their frequency. Finally, Gord explained to the taxi company who we were and what was going on and asked if we could, with their permission, use their radio frequency for the next half-hour. They kindly agreed.

It was decided to evacuate the person in the worst shape. There was no question that was me. Now instead of being left behind, I was going to be the first one to be carried off the mountain.

To do the rescue, they needed minimum weight because of the altitude. So I had to empty my pockets. I had to dump everything. I only carried two things off the mountain with me: the picture of my daughter I'd never met and a Spyderco, police-edition knife that I'd had since I was about 18.

Once I had dumped most of my stuff, they hooked up a harness to a basket that Jim had dropped a couple of metres (5 ft) from the tent. I had no power to walk on my own, so they had to carry me, one under each arm, and they threw me in the basket.

I could not hold on because my hands were frozen, so I gripped one of the ropes in the crook of each elbow and that was the best I could do. They attached me to the rescue basket by my climbing harness, and after checking that I was secured they backed away so the Lama could carry me down.

Next thing I knew I heard the helicopter engine howl, and I was lifted about an inch off the icy ground and then dropped down again. I started to worry that maybe I was too heavy. I was definitely the biggest of us three. Then I was picked up only about half an inch and once again dropped back down. And the next attempt didn't lift me at all. Tears pricked at my eyes. I was too heavy. We were too high. Whatever the reason or combinations of reasons, I was not going to make it off the mountain after all. It was clear the Lama did not have the power to pick me up.

I waited for Gord to come and unhook me from the

harness. But my friends were still standing a fair distance off. I wondered if they just hadn't been paying attention. Before I could finish processing that thought, however, my harness jerked and I started to be pulled sideways toward the cliff. Panic shot through me. The Lama started to pick up speed. I was heading straight for a couple-thousand-foot drop.

I didn't know if Jim could see me, or if he even knew he was doing this. I started screaming.

I was being dragged along the ice toward the cliff. My heart leapt to my throat and my mind went blank. I couldn't do anything. I was fastened to the basket by my harness. Just when I thought I would survive this ordeal, was I about to be killed in the rescue attempt? I looked back at my friends, and they were just watching me go. They didn't look concerned at all. They almost looked as if they were wondering why I was freaking out. But there was nothing they could do anyway.

Then I was over the cliff and falling. I screamed again as the basket dropped and my weight pulled the helicopter down. For I moment I thought Jim was going to go down with me, but then suddenly I was being lifted.

Relief poured through me. I took a great gulp of frozen air and tried to process what had just happened. Then I realized that the drop must have created more air pressure underneath the rotors. Jim Hood knew exactly what he was doing. The fact that we were on a ledge probably worked better for the rescue attempt – the Lama did not have to try to lift us up, it could just drag us off the mountain.

After my heartbeat slowed down, I slowly became aware

of my location. You would think that it would be loud and windy with the helicopter carrying me away, but it wasn't; it was calm.

As we flew down the valley, a surge of such joy and peace filtered through me it was almost exhilarating. Because we were so far north it was still light out, even though it was near midnight by now. There was a pink alpine glow that infused everything. I was struck by the beauty surrounding me.

It was almost as if I were in a dream state. The pain in my hands was momentarily forgotten as the rugged beauty of the mountains filled me with a joyfulness that I almost couldn't contain. I was going to live. And this was definitely something worth living for.

For the first time in three days, I knew that survival would prevail over death.

We flew down to a staging area at 3800 metres (12,500 ft), and the military was waiting for me. The next hour or so passed in a flurry of activity. I was given food and something hot to drink, and I accepted the supplies in a state of shock. I didn't really register what was going on. It must have taken about 20 minutes to fly me down, and then Jim turned around and did the same thing for Don and Alex. As soon as my friends were safe beside me I knew we were all going to live.

18 Realizations

*"There is nothing you can't do, if you
set your mind to it. Anything is possible."*

—RICK HANSEN

May 28–June 1, 2005 – Anchorage, Alaska

I woke in the hospital in Anchorage, disoriented and float-
ing on a cocktail of painkillers and other medications.
In my memory, those first few days after rescue, perhaps
the first several weeks – I don't really know – are a blur of
faces, voices and pain. The one thing that remained clear in
my mind was an overarching thankfulness that I had
survived.

Alex and Don were both severely hypothermic and de-
hydrated. They had suffered frostbite as well, but not as
badly as I had. Don's toes were severely frostbitten. We
weren't sure if he would lose them or not. But Alex and
Don were able to come to my room in their wheelchairs
and visit with me.

183

Slowly the pieces of what had happened after Jim Hood carried us down the mountain came together. At Base Camp, the Alaska Air Guard was waiting for us. When Don and Alex were successfully brought down the mountain, the Air Guard flew the three of us to Anchorage via the Pave Hawk helicopters. I will forever be indebted to the highly skilled and professional U.S. military pilots and Jim Hood.

Even though we were all Canadian citizens and climbing in Canada, it was decided that Anchorage was the best place for immediate medical care. Because Kluane Park is so remote, there is no hospital on the Canadian side of the border that could provide the intensive care that we needed. Alaska Regional Hospital is well known for cutting-edge frostbite and hypothermia treatment. Dr. James O'Malley is renowned for his expertise in treating frostbite patients. So it was decided early on that we would be transported there if we were successfully rescued.

I do have vague memories of the flight to Anchorage. I remember lying in the back of the Pave Hawk and the surreality of it all. I had not slept in more than three days. I was so tired, and I was now feeling the full effects of hypothermia. I started to hallucinate and see things that could not have been there. At one point, I saw a pack of beautiful grey wolves running along the trees as if they were following us out of the mountains. It was not possible that I could have really seen that, but it was a beautiful vision.

It was 1:30 a.m. when Don and Alex were finally safely lifted off the mountain. It was the darkest it gets at that time of year up there. The pilots shut off all the interior lights on the Pave Hawk and they put down their visors and had their night vision on. Don and Alex were with me in the helicopter but we did not talk. I don't think we said more than ten words. I don't know if it was because we were too weak or in shock or if it was that we were too amazed that we had actually survived. Maybe we were scared to talk because we thought we were dreaming.

We were in Anchorage from May 27 until June 1.

I felt extremely grateful. I was just so thankful that I was alive. I couldn't explain why we had lived. But I knew there must be a reason for it all, one I didn't understand yet. Even though I was grateful, as I slowly started to regain my grip on reality, I started to worry. Ironically, the first thing that I worried about was not my hands but the financial situation I was sure to find myself in.

I was a Canadian, and I had been evacuated from Canada to an American hospital in an American military aircraft. Every Canadian knows that if you travel outside of Canada, you need to purchase travel insurance in case you get hurt. I'd travelled the world for years, and I'd always purchased medical insurance when I left my country. But not when I went to Logan. We were climbing in Canada, after all. I never imagined that I would find myself in Alaska needing medical treatment. I began to think, "Oh, there goes my house, my car, everything." I started to worry that I would be paying back this debt for the rest of my life.

When they first brought us out of the helicopter and took us into the hospital, I remember being so embarrassed.

When they asked me if I had insurance, I would have had to say no. I had heard all these horrible stories about healthcare costs in American hospitals. I thought they would just push us out into the alley.

But they did not mention insurance at all. They took us to the most amazing, private hospital rooms. When they put me in the bed, I sank into paradise and forgot about my worries for a while. It was the first time I had been in a comfortable bed in about a month. My hands were excruciatingly painful, but it was bearable. I remember thinking this is it. I lived through it. This is truly a miracle.

As I drifted in and out of consciousness over the first few days, I remember occasionally waking and finding all kinds of people around me. Doctors, nurses and other medical personnel were the most prominent. At first when I heard them talking to each other I was confused because I thought they were speaking in a different language. But I think I was just so exhausted that I could not even understand English. Regardless, I felt incredibly safe and well cared for at the time.

When I finally regained consciousness, I soon realized how badly injured I actually was. I could not get up to see Alex or Don. The nurses would wheel them into my room to visit with me every now and then. While they were there, we would laugh and talk. I think we were all still shell shocked, amazed that we had actually survived the ordeal.

During my time in the hospital, I had the best treatment possible for deep frostbite wounds and hypothermia. Twice a day I was taken to a room with a special whirlpool in it. There I soaked my hands in a special tub for 20 minutes to gradually warm the deep tissues. It was excruciatingly painful, but the nurses and doctors told me it would help, so I did it. I was willing to do anything I could to save my hands.

When I regained some strength, the staff started to get me out of bed. I still had to continue with the whirlpool treatments for my hands twice a day. I would place my hands in the hot tub and try to ignore the burning pain that dominated those sessions.

I could not escape the damage that had been done to my hands. The hot baths were unbelievably painful. The heat just burned and burned. They told me it would help so I did whatever I could because I was so terrified about losing my hands past my wrists. I felt I would most likely lose both my hands.

I knew that my life had been irrevocably changed but how dramatically was yet to be determined. In the early days, the doctors were very close lipped. They were in wait-and-see mode, not wanting to commit to any prognosis. The true extent of frostbite injures is not something that can be predicted quickly, hence the adage, "Frostbite in January, amputate in July." So I held on to the hope that my hands could be saved. I did not want to rule out any possibility. At the same time, I was not under any illusion that I would get out of this unscathed. All I had to do was look at my fingers to see that serious damage had been done to them.

Within a few days, huge blisters began to form on my fingers and they became dark purple. Soon, they darkened even more until they were deep black, and my fingernails started to turn yellow and fall off. The smell that radiated from them told me that the flesh was dead, but the doctors weren't quick to dismiss my hands.

Because I was still immersing my hands in the daily baths, they weren't bandaged, and I just lay in my hospital bed and stared at them. It was as if they belonged to someone else. My own hands had never looked like this. Swollen and black and oozing pus. They were disgusting, and part of me was so revolted that I wanted them gone.

No. I didn't want my hands gone – I just wanted my old hands back. I didn't want what I was seeing: those black fingers that sounded like hollow wood when I tapped them together. They couldn't be a part of me, could they?

Before too many days had passed, the smell was overpowering. The putrid, slightly sweet smell of rotting flesh. My hands reeked of death, and yet I was still alive. And because I was alive, I had to keep functioning. I had to feed myself with these disgusting, stinking appendages. It was enough to put me off my food.

While I received treatment in Alaska, many friends and family members were doing what they could to take my mind off my situation and to raise my spirits. The Firefighters Union sent one of my closest friends and fellow firefighter, Dave Dorey, to come up to the hospital and give me moral support, which was really nice. I remember the look on Dave's face when he first saw my hands. He quickly cleared his face of all emotion, but not before I saw the shock and sorrow in his eyes.

My parents were among the first people I spoke to. They were beyond relieved that I was safe, and they wanted to fly up to Alaska to be with me. However, with all the attention from the media and the visitors I was getting, I did not see the point in them going to the expense and trouble of flying up to Alaska. I knew I would be relying on them when I arrived in Vancouver, and part of me did not really want them to see the extent of my injuries quite yet.

In addition to the support from my buddies, I was getting so much media attention. We did not know it at the time, but our story had made national headlines in Canada when we were trapped on Logan. Part of this was because we were on NSR's 40th anniversary climb, part of it was because we were rescue workers and part of it was because we were trapped in a life-and-death situation on Canada's highest peak. When we were rescued, just when everyone (including ourselves) thought that we would not make it, the media jumped on our story with even more enthusiasm.

There were many reporters at the hospital, and as soon as I was well enough to visit with people, I started giving interviews. When I look back on it now, I realize I probably should not have done those interviews. I was on a lot of painkillers to try to control the extreme pain I was in, and half the time I do not think I even knew what I was saying. Some of what I said was really funny, but I do regret some of the other stuff I said.

One of the reporters asked what I was going to do next. It was a ridiculous question. There was no way at that stage that even my doctors could have predicted what I would and would not have been able to do. I still had not come to terms with the damage that my hands had suffered. But when you are asked a question on live television, you feel compelled to answer it.

I said that I was hoping I would be able to come back to my work as a firefighter, my dream job. The reporter was not satisfied with that answer (maybe sensing the lack of reality there) and pushed me, asking what I would do if that were not possible. That was such a deeply personal question. One I had not even fully processed myself. One I had not discussed with my family or even my closest friends. Yet the reporters expected an answer from me. I told them I supposed I could hold a position in the fire-prevention unit. I should have just left it at that, but the extreme disappointment I felt at the possibility of losing my career prodded me to add that if I had to do that, I would rather have been left on the mountain to die.

Unfortunately, I said that during a live interview. I said it as a joke but also because I had not wanted to consider what my options were quite yet. If I had said it in the fire hall kitchen or with a group of my buddies, maybe it would have been funny. But to say it on live TV was unforgiveable. It was an insult to every fire-prevention officer out there. And the truth is I have a great deal of respect for those officers. Their job is just as valuable as mine was as a firefighter; I just was not prepared to face alternatives to my career as a front-line worker, or to accept that I might have to at that stage.

Firefighters are family. No matter where you are in the world, if you are in trouble, other firefighters will seek you out and offer their assistance. This was probably most publicly brought into view during the 9/11 attacks in New York. Firefighters from all over the world offered their support to the NYC battalions.

In Alaska, a similar thing happened to me. Because I was all over the news, the local firemen started stopping by my hospital room in Anchorage. At least twice a day a firefighter would come in for a quick visit and to raise my spirits. Words will never describe how grateful I was for the tremendous support I received from the military, firefighters and medical personnel in Alaska.

I was greatly surprised when NSR team leader Tim Jones walked into my hospital room the day after the rescue. I thought maybe I was hallucinating again. He laughed at my reaction. Tim had wasted no time in flying up to check on us. He arrived with Bridget Milsom, another senior member of the rescue team.

Their timing could not have been better, because while Don, Alex and I were safe and recuperating in Anchorage, we had been getting more and more concerned about Gord Ferguson and Linda Bily. They had stayed on the mountain when we were airlifted off and opted to climb down on their own. Conditions on the mountain were such that while it was possible for them to climb out we were still worried about them. On May 30 we heard that Gord, Linda, Barry and Isabel had finally made it safely off the mountain. That was cause for celebration.

Gord later told me that he had been overcome with exhaustion after we were carried off the mountain. After they watched the Lama leave for the final time, he and Linda turned back to the tent where we had been sheltered for the previous 12 hours. Gord said it looked like they had hosted a frat party.

Everything was wet, with frost crystals growing on the walls. All of their gear had been dispersed to cover five people, and spills were everywhere. After we left, there was a shortage of everything, as all of their emergency supplies had been used.

But the relief over the rescue muted any inconvenience we had caused. Gord and Linda were just so relieved that it was over. They quickly reorganized the tent as best they could, and Gord says he fell into a dreamless sleep the moment his head hit his rolled-up jacket.

The following day the fine weather held, and they headed down the mountain. With all the snow left in the wake of the storm, they had to engage in some significant route finding as they worked their way up and then down off the col. Gord acknowledged that the ramp down proved to be unpleasant, stating that the main route down looked totally unfamiliar as they skied toward the cache lower on the route.

With the new snow more than a metre (3 ft) deep, Gord had to break trail downhill to make progress on the less-steep sections. When they got to the appointed spot, they had to dig 2 metres (6 ft) down to expose their cache. They then had plenty of groceries and fuel.

Gord later told me that there were some interesting moments getting off King Col in crappy snow conditions, but he was determined to get off the steeper terrain and into the col. There was sensible talk of waiting for it to cool and see if the slope would firm up, but Gord wanted to get home. He said he snapped and just sent the sled straight down the slope as an avalanche assessment. Thankfully, it worked, and also made skiing down easier.

On their last day down, they hit another whiteout below King Col and had to face an open crevasse field in zero visibility. Things had changed dramatically since our ascent. The fog was so thick and the route had changed so much that Gord was relieved when Barry and Isabel came up the glacier, on radio and roped up, to guide them to Base Camp. The weather finally cleared and they all left Base Camp on the first flights out the following morning.

After hearing Gord's story, we had even more cause for celebration, and I hosted a small party for Tim, Dave, Alex and Don, featuring plenty of Scotch and beer.

I had many really nice distractions to keep my mind off what was happening with my hands while I was in Alaska. While I was in the hospital I also met a lot of people, folks who had just seen the news and would come in and talk to me. So I felt that I had tremendous support. Those distractions did help, even though I knew that I would eventually have to face facts about my hands.

This was an extremely emotional time for me, especially when I took on some difficult phone conversations. It had not been so long ago that I was passing along my farewell messages to Barry. I had truly believed that I would die on that mountain, and now I had things to tell to the people I loved.

My mom has always had the ability to break me down to a child. When she called, I told her how much I loved her. I talked to my father. I knew I had probably taken about ten years off his life when they thought they had lost me.

My family had believed that they *had* lost me. The Bjarnasons are a tight-knit clan, and news of my plight had spread quickly. So when my folks started hearing that we were stuck on the mountain, it wasn't long before all my uncles and cousins knew I was in trouble.

With the loss of the satellite phone, there was very little information coming off the mountain to our families back home. Tim Jones had been honest with my parents and told them it didn't look good, and so they started to prepare for the worst, probably because there was nothing else they felt they could do. Getting that kind of news about your child must be devastating.

While we were surviving on the mountain, my family had been thinking about funerals and trying to figure out the logistics of getting my body back to them. I'm sure it was a horrifying time for them.

As well, because the news was shocking and devastating, it also became dramatized, embellished with every call to a family member, to the point that by the 30th call, I was going to be dead in the next ten minutes. As a result, my parents were getting many support and sympathy calls from family members, which was a bit premature.

In hindsight, we probably should have died. In many ways that was what should have happened. When I reflect on it now, I am still surprised that we survived. It was blind fate, incredible luck and the amazing dedication of many individuals on the mountain that saved us.

19   The Teddy Bear

*"Life is a series of natural and spontaneous
changes. Don't resist them – that only creates sorrow.
Let reality be reality. Let things flow naturally
forward in whatever way they like."*

—LAO TZU

May 28–June 1, 2005 – Anchorage, Alaska

As time passed in the hospital, I started thinking about
when I would be able to return home. Alex and Don were
discharged from the hospital on May 31 and given the okay
to return home, but the doctors weren't ready for me to
leave at that point. My friends, ever generous, decided to
wait for me.

I wanted to see my family. I wanted to hold my kids
again. The hospital had grown old very quickly, and I just
wanted to go home. But until the doctors were satisfied that
it was safe to transfer me to Vancouver, I was stuck where
I was.

As I sat in my hospital bed, I continued to worry about

mounting medical bills. Was I going to be permanently scarred, unable to work and in terrible debt for the rest of my life? As it turned out, all my fears were unfounded. To my surprise, I discovered that I actually did have travel insurance. My extended Blue Cross medical benefits through my employer actually covered all of my treatments in Alaska.

My financial good luck continued. The Alaska Air Guard had used our rescue as a training mission. As we were ourselves SAR professionals and had paid insurance at Kluane before we started our Logan climb, our government at home covered the cost of the Lama helicopter. It turned out I did not have to pay a penny. I hated to reduce my situation to money, but I also had to be practical. I had a very uncertain future ahead of me, and I had children to care for. To have the financial burden lifted was a blessing. It allowed me to focus on getting better.

As I rested in the hospital, I received many messages. Most of them were supportive, and it really lifted my spirits to get messages from so many strangers who were pulling for me. But there was, of course, some hate mail in the mix. There were people who said we should not have been up there in the first place and that it was a waste of money to rescue us. I can understand that way of thinking, but no one could be as hard on myself as I was. With each day it was becoming more and more apparent that I was going to pay the ultimate price for my climbing addiction.

I know much of the public does not understand the need and desire to climb. People are quick to judge. But the truth is we *were* prepared for our climb on Logan. We did everything right. Sometimes in mountaineering luck is not on your side and can turn on the most experienced and well-equipped climbers.

In certain respects, luck certainly did not seem to be on my side now. The more days I spent in the hospital, the worse my hands were looking, and I was getting more and more worried. My fingers, in addition to having gone completely black and smelling worse and worse, didn't hurt anymore, which I knew was a bad sign. It was clear to me that those fingers had died. I didn't understand why the doctors were so reluctant to amputate. But I had a lot to learn about the treatment of frostbite.

I thought the amputations would start right away, but the modern medical process does not work like that. In the past, they did just remove the part of the body that appeared to have died. Modern technology, however, allows medical practitioners to take more time in deciding what to amputate. In the past, sometimes patients would lose more than they had to. Or the doctors would not remove enough, and then they would have to go in later and take more tissue.

It was revolting in a way that is hard to imagine. I had to live with these dead and rotting appendages, and at the same time, I had no idea how much of my fingers I was going to lose. Of course, I was hoping that I would only lose the very tips, but that didn't look likely because the black was down almost to the anchor knuckles on my left hand and pretty much to the second knuckles on my right hand.

I tried to keep reminding myself of the positives. The

doctors had told me that I would only lose my fingers. Of course, this was definitely a huge loss but at the same time much better than losing my whole arm up to my elbow, which was what I had originally feared would be the case.

While there was a certain amount of wait and see from the medical personnel, they also conducted many tests that measure blood flow – angiography, thermography and x-ray – to determine the level of the damage. One of the main indicators of tissue that will survive is blood flow. Where there is blood flow, there is viable tissue, and where there is no blood flow, the tissue is dead.

The afternoon I got the final results of the tests, I was nervous. I had an x-ray that showed what was left of my hands. As I sat with my doctor, Dr. O'Malley, and looked at the results on the bright x-ray screen my gut clenched. All the fingers of my left hand were basically gone. There was no blood flow at all in those fingers. My right hand didn't look much better. All my fingers were affected down to the second knuckle.

I stared at the cold hard evidence in front of me. My mind tried to reject what I had already known deep down. I was essentially going to be fingerless. The room started to close in on me, and I started to breathe hard. What was I going to do with my life? How could I do even the most basic thing with no fingers? Sure, it was great to have my hands but hands with no fingers...what good were those?

Negative thoughts started to float through my head. "I won't be able to pick up a beer can. I won't be able to write. I won't be able to even dress myself." I just sat there and stared at the x-ray and thought, "Oh, my God, what have

I done to myself? My life is going to be over. I'm going to have to have people help to do everything. My independence is gone." I thought I would have to move back in with my parents, ruin their lives as they became full-time caregivers to me.

I choked back tears as despair threatened to pull me under. Dr. O'Malley said some reassuring words, but I didn't hear him. I was levelled by what he'd shown me. I returned to my room not really seeing where I was going. I just wanted to be alone in my misery. As I climbed back into my hospital bed, someone breezed into my room with another delivery. I'd been getting gifts on a regular basis, but this one was odd enough that it momentarily jarred me from my misery. It was a little teddy bear. I stared at it through my tears, dumbfounded. "What the hell?" I wondered.

It was one of the weirdest gifts I'd received, and I tried to imagine who would send a 40-year old, 220-lb firefighter a stuffed bear. The absurdity of it, in the midst of such horrific news, slammed me.

There was a little note attached to bear with a plastic holder. I squinted at it, and slowly the words came together and made sense. It said: *Hi, my name's Joline. I'm your daughter. I'd like to talk to you.* And it had a phone number on it.

I stared at it for a good minute, disbelief flooding me. Then my heart started pounding as I remembered how I'd believed that I would never get a chance to meet my oldest daughter. She had found me. And more than that, she wanted to speak to me. For a minute I forgot about the rotting fingers holding her note. I went in search of a phone. I found my buddy, Dave Dorey, and got him to put the call through for me. I waited through two rings before someone picked up. It was Joline's mom.

Davina told me that they'd been following my story on the news. She said that Joline had been especially upset by my situation because she had actually asked her mom if she could contact me just two days before we had got trapped on Logan. Her mom had said yes.

This was such a huge decision for her, and I am sure it was not an easy one. She must have been apprehensive and scared to look up the father she had never known. Then, just as she had come to the decision to track me down, the front page of the *Vancouver Sun* announced that I was going to die. She was pretty devastated. She had waited her whole life to meet me, and now it appeared that I had gone and got myself killed on a mountain.

When I had survived and been rescued, it was such a miracle for her. She hadn't hesitated to send that little stuffed bear right away.

When Joline came to the phone, she sounded a bit shy and hesitant at first, which was only to be expected. After all, she didn't really know me. But after just a few minutes of chatting she warmed up to me. We ended up having this fantastic talk.

Joline couldn't know how important that talk was to me. It had come at a time when I was feeling the absolute lowest I had since being lifted off the mountain. The teddy bear she sent arrived at the perfect moment. After our conversation I almost forgot the dark thoughts I'd been having after seeing my x-rays. Instead I focused on getting a chance to build a relationship with my beautiful daughter. And just like that one of my worst days turned into one of my best.

After I spoke to Joline, I remembered what Dr. O'Malley had told me while we were looking at the x-ray. My dismay must have blocked out his words at the time, but now that I was calmer they came back to me. He told me not to panic. He said I would be amazed by what I would be able to do with what I had. He said, "Let's wait and see what you're capable of. The only one who can limit what you can do is yourself."

As it turned out, that was the best advice I could have received

20 No Limits

*"Have the courage to follow your heart
and your intuition. They somehow already
know what you truly want to become."*

—STEVE JOBS

Summer 2005 – Vancouver

I would like to say life got back to normal when I arrived
back in Vancouver on June 1, but it did not. Not for me.
After a while the media frenzy settled down, my buddies
recovered and went back to their lives, and I sat in the hospital, not knowing what the future would bring for me.

After the plane landed at Vancouver International Airport, I was transported via ambulance to the Burn Unit at
Vancouver General Hospital. I spent the next few months
there. When people ask me about that part of my life, it
is hard to describe. All I can really say is that, despite the
kindness I was given by so many people, it really was a
dead time in my life.

It didn't take long for me to become bored out of my mind. Normally I am a very active person. I spend most of my free time outside. Now I was confined to a hospital bed. I was also on a lot of painkillers, and they were pretty powerful. If I am honest, I would have to say I do not remember much, but I do remember the tedious days. They melted into one another, and before long a dark depression began to weigh down on me. Despite my dark moods, one thing that never failed to lift my spirits was the number of visitors I had, and for that I will always be grateful. I did not really start to heal, not emotionally, in that time. If anything, I just floated along, waiting for my life to get back on track.

Of course, I was thankful for so much, and I was able to reflect on that while I was hospitalized. I did get to hold my children again. Ariyah and Shayman were waiting for me at the airport, and any doubt I might have had about them knowing how much I cared was quickly dispelled. They were so happy to see me. They would come to my hospital room and sit up on the bed with me, and we would just hug each other. I thanked God on a daily basis that I was able to once again hold my children.

Not long after I arrived in Vancouver, I finally got to meet Joline. But our meeting wasn't as I had hoped it would be. It was tainted with what had happened on Logan. Our first meeting should have been a special, private moment. But it wasn't. Somehow the media had received word of what was happening and, ever ready to sell another paper, a crowd of reporters and cameras descended on the hospital the day Joline arrived. I look back now at the video of that meeting, and I can see how overwhelmed she was. I can only imagine how nervous she must have been to meet the father she had never known, and then when she arrived she was greeted with flashbulbs and questions from the press. It should have a quiet family moment, but it turned into a media circus.

During the summer I had what seemed like a never-ending series of surgeries. I soon lost count of how many procedures were required. In a way it didn't matter to me because it had become abundantly clear that I would lose all my fingers. It must have taken about a dozen surgeries on my hands to get them to where they are today.

At one point, the doctors approached me with an option that could make my right hand a bit more useable. They said that if they surgically inserted my hand into my abdomen, I might get a bit more flesh on my hand because the bones weren't completely dead. At that stage I would try anything that might give me more useable fingers. So an abdominal flap was wrapped around my fingers. This procedure is used often for any degloved-hand injury (where the bone is intact but the flesh and skin is no longer viable). The aim was to save as much of my right fingers as possible. And it was a relatively successful procedure. I ended up with a few more centimetres on my right hand than my left. And with what I was losing, every centimetre counted.

During the summer my life revolved around the hospital and surgeries. Because I was going so stir crazy in the hospital, I talked them in to giving me "day passes." I could leave the hospital for the day and come back for my treatments and to sleep each night. Although I couldn't do too much when I was out for the day, at least I got out of the constant hospital buzz.

As summer leached into fall, I was finally released from the hospital for good. And then it was up to me to get my life back together. Or to at least to try and figure out what kind of life I was going to have. I became determined to retain my independence and to avoid being a burden to anyone.

Of course, at first I was a complete invalid. I could not even feed myself. But I worked hard with an occupational therapist and a physiotherapist. They gave me little exercises to practice, but the tasks seemed so small. Many of the activities they had me do were aimed at toughening up my fingers. Although they had sewn skin over the bone tips of what was left of my fingers, the sensitivity of the stubs was extreme. Pain would shoot up my arms with the slightest touch. At first, it was excruciatingly painful to use them for anything.

One exercise I was taught in therapy involved dragging my hand through a shallow pan of sand once an hour to help desensitize my fingers; at first, it was painful. The pain would radiate up my arm, and it was almost unbearable.

The doctors were brutally honest with me. They told me that I was looking at two to three years before I would be able to be self-sufficient. After they delivered this news, I sat in my chair and stared at the wall. How had I gone from being an extremely active and involved community member to an invalid? I couldn't believe that it would take so long to recover. I thought to myself, "Holy cow, two to three years!"

Then the anger came. So I was supposed to sit around on my butt, dragging my hands through a pile of sand, and in two years maybe I would be able to care for myself? That was insane! And it was so discouraging. I thought, "No way. There has to be some way to speed up this process."

Truth be told, I was still holding out the hope that I would get my job back at the fire department. I did not advertise the fact, because I did not want to be laughed at. I wasn't thinking of a desk position or taking on a job as a fire-prevention officer. I wanted my former job back. I really believed that I had what it took to go back to fighting fires. I felt in my soul that I was meant to be a firefighter. Anything else just did not feel right. I wasn't ready to just settle into a life that was limited by my injuries.

I decided to take everything I had learned in life and use it to try to find a way to overcome this challenge. As I've said before, one of my defining characteristics is my stubbornness and my ability to rise to any challenge. This was a challenge I was determined to meet head on.

I thought back to my former experiences, trying to think of something that could help me now. I remembered one of my trips to China. While there I had immersed myself as much as possible in the culture and so I had taken the opportunity to study martial arts. I stayed in the Shaolin Monastery in rural China and one of the things we did was to dig our knuckles into uncooked rice on a daily basis to toughen up our knuckles. I wondered if that could work for me again in the situation I was in.

When I got out of the hospital, I renounced the sand tray, deciding I would toughen up my fingers with rice. I found an Asian supermarket that was happy to give me all the rice it couldn't sell: split bags, for example. I took the rice home, put it in a bowl and sat in front of the TV. Then I dug my fingers into it and twisted my hand just as we had done with our knuckles at the monastery. The first time I did it, the pain was so intense I saw dark spots in my vision and thought I was going to vomit. But I focused my mind and did it again. And then again.

Every time I plunged my hand into the bowl, pain would shoot up my arm, making me gasp. But I would force myself to keep doing it. I reminded myself of the alternative: life as an invalid. And then I'd dig my hand in again and again. Soon tears would roll down my cheeks, and the stumps of my fingers would bleed. But I refused to give up; I would take a deep breath and keep going.

The next day I did the same thing, and the scabs that had started to form on the tips of my fingers would split open and fresh blood would ooze out. But I ignored it and continued the exercise. After a few months of this I was able to make the tips of my fingers as tough as my elbows, and then I could do anything with them.

When they first amputated my fingers, it felt very awkward, much like when you lose a tooth and you feel for it with your tongue, sometimes unconsciously, and you are surprised by the lack of it there. My hands were like that. I would reach for my glass and then suddenly realize there were no fingers to grasp it.

But humans adapt. Even the most debilitating injuries can be adapted to. It is called survival. I learned how to do everything differently. I learned tricks to make my life easier. Take beer mugs, for example. When I pick up a beer mug now, I manoeuvre what is left of my pinky finger underneath the mug to give it stability, which makes up for my shortened hand. The funny thing is that, now, many people don't even notice my hands at first. It sounds strange but it's true. In social situations I've noticed that it takes some people up to an hour to notice that I don't have any fingers.

For a long time after losing my fingers I was kind of ashamed of my hands. I would always have them in my pockets. At first I didn't go out as much as I used to. I sat in my apartment and drank Jack Daniels.

Then one morning a couple weeks after going home, I woke up and looked at the half-empty bottle on my kitchen table and I wondered what I was doing with my life. I could sit down in front of the television with a glass of whiskey and a bowl of uncooked rice and feel sorry for myself, or I could do something about it. I looked out the window to the coniferous forest that cloaks Seymour Mountain, and I asked myself what the hell I was doing. I had Mother Nature at my back door, and I had been staying inside feeling sorry for myself.

In that moment I decided I was going to get back to my former self. I was going to do all the things I loved to do. The doctors weren't going to put limits on me. I remembered what Dr. O'Malley in Alaska had told me: only *you* will determine how much you can or cannot do.

21 | Getting My Life Back

*"I'd rather attempt to do something great
and fail, than to attempt nothing and succeed."*

—ROBERT H. SCHULLER

January 2006 – North Vancouver

After the doctors told me it would be two years until I could feed and take care of myself, I could have fallen into a deep depression. And if I'm honest, I will say that I almost did. But that one morning's realization, when I really saw what my life might become, made me determined to get my old life back. I was determined to be a firefighter.

Since I had decided that I would get my regular job back, I started hanging out at the fire hall again. I had been by to visit the guys after I was first released from the hospital, but now I started showing up as if I actually was going to work. I quickly let it be known that I planned to come back. I think it was a shock for my coworkers. I think they really did not know what to do with me at first because my injuries were so obvious. I don't think anyone really believed that I could do it.

If I could not do the job, I would have quit gracefully. I would have found something else to do with my life. But I knew in my heart that I *could* do it. Before this I had been outspoken about hiring females into the fire department. I had made it clear that I did not think they should be hired if they could not do the job. I did not say this as a statement against women; I feel that one should not be a firefighter if one cannot do the work, regardless of one's gender.

I know firsthand that there are women who can definitely do the job. There are several women in the fire department who are stronger than I am. These women are probably more outspoken about job fit than I am because they do not want to work beside another woman who got the position as a result of an equal-opportunity hiring process and not because of her ability.

Being a firefighter is a physically demanding job. It requires a strong person to do what we do. If you are not strong enough, then you put yourself, your fellow members *and* the general public in danger. The bottom line for me is that there are women and men who can do the job, and there are men and women who cannot do the job. I was determined to prove that I was still one of the ones who could do the job.

When I came back and announced my intentions, there were mixed reactions. About 5 per cent of the firefighters did not believe I could do it, and it seemed as though they almost hated me for even trying to get my job back. I think a few of them wished that I would just go away and die. But about 90 per cent of the firefighters were not so quick to judge me. They knew me from before Logan, and they also knew it took a pretty tough individual to get through everything I had gone through. They decided to just wait and see.

The final 5 per cent of them just wanted the department to give me my job back. But that would not have been right. Even though I wasn't ready to admit it, there was a chance that I might not be able to do the job again, and reinstating me without any proof of my ability would put far too many lives in danger. There is a reason we have a fair process for qualifying for the job.

I think many of the firefighters were hoping I could do it. They understood that I wanted my job back. But at the same time, if I could not do the job they would have been 100 per cent for getting rid of me. I think I would have felt exactly the same way. Cut him loose if he can't prove himself worthy. At least, I hope I would have felt that way. I don't want to work beside a guy who is just a token fireman because he is a good guy and he used to be able to do the job. Heck, I certainly did not want to be that guy; the guy everybody hides, who is told to sit in the truck on calls because the capable firefighters are concerned about disaster resulting from him trying to do his job.

I wanted to prove to myself and to my colleagues that I could do the job. I wanted to show everyone, including myself, that I could be just as good a firefighter as I was before Logan. Of course, I knew I was in for a difficult challenge and not just physically. Generally speaking, the attitudes of the chiefs – those who would ultimately decide whether or not I could come back to my job – were very similar to those of the firefighters at the hall; most of them were prepared to give me a chance. However, it seemed to me that one chief in particular wanted me gone. He seemed to think it was a joke that I wanted my job back; and it seemed to me that he went out of his way to make it difficult for me.

Unfortunately, I think this chief had decided that I could not do the job before I even had a chance to prove myself. I was still sure I could do it, and so I asked to be tested, just as any new recruit would have to be. He did not like that. I think he felt it was a total waste of his time. The look he gave me spelled it out: I would be useless on the job and someone with such catastrophic injuries could not realistically be a firefighter. I could understand this way of thinking. It seemed almost impossible that I would be able to do it. But I couldn't understand his apparent reluctance to let me even try. He seemed so sure I would fail. His doubt, however, strengthened my determination to prove him and others wrong. More that anything, I needed to prove to myself that I could overcome the odds that were stacked sky high against me.

It must have been a strange position for the department to be in. I qualified for long-term disability for the rest of my working life, and a lot of guys who had suffered an injury like mine would have been happy with that. But for me, being a firefighter is not just a career, it is my identity. I needed to do the job to be me.

The firefighters are unionized, and the union determined that I was entitled to the opportunity to test. In the end, the doubting fire chief had no choice but to let me test. But he did not seem happy about it. He told me that if I could pass the same tests as any new recruit would have to go through, then I could have my job back.

He had to let me take the tests, but he did not make the approach easy. The chief didn't want to spend any effort on me. He wasn't going to waste any of his own energy in helping me prepare for the testing. Every day I would go to him and ask what I should work on, but instead of giving me some real exercises to practice, he would just tell me to go in the other room and read. The first time this happened I was angry. My eyes were fine and there was nothing I needed to read to do my job better. I had been a firefighter for almost 20 years! But I knew that showing my anger would not help me. So I swallowed it down and instead trained myself in preparation for the tests. The more difficult an exercise was, the more I would work on it so I could master it.

It was tough. At times I could hear the guys laughing when they didn't know I was there, and I tried not to take it to heart. I felt almost betrayed. After all, we are supposed to be this great family and some guys are laughing at me behind my back and saying things like, "What's he doing? He can't even wipe his ass and he wants to be a fireman?" and "Well, he wasn't much of a fireman before so this shouldn't make much of a difference." I like to hope that I would not have said such things if I was in their spot, but I suppose you never know unless you are in that position.

I had to rethink how to do even the most basic task. I spent hours trying to figure out how I could perform my duties without fingers. Some days I was so discouraged I actually asked myself what I was doing. But the next morning I would get up and go to the fire hall and start training all over again. There was a drive deep inside me that told me I was doing the right thing.

While I was getting myself ready to retest for my job, I felt like I was in limbo. I wasn't really a firefighter, but I wasn't a civilian. Most of the guys made me feel welcome, but at times I felt I was outside looking in. And even though I had worked at the fire hall for almost 20 years, the place felt strange to me.

On the days I wasn't at work, I was in the forest, hiking and slowly building up my stamina. All the stress and depression that at times threatened to consume me disappeared when I was on those hikes. And slowly I began to be able to do longer and longer day hikes. I could feel my former self coming back.

It took a long time for me to accomplish even the smallest improvement. I reminded myself of how I'd been told by the doctors that I wouldn't be self-sufficient for three years. And here I was living on my own, hiking in the woods and training to get my job back. I should have felt that I'd accomplished a lot, but I still had bouts of deep depression.

Then came a day when I was feeling really down. It all just seemed like too much, and I really did question what I was doing with my life. I looked at where my fingers had been. They were now healed but what remained looked almost hideous to me. I wondered how anyone could ever see me as anything more than a freak. It was at this point that I was hiding my hands in my pockets when I wasn't using them for something. I hated the stares and whispers from strangers.

Then out of the blue I got a call from the burn ward at Vancouver General Hospital. I had been there for so long the summer before, and I'd made friends with many of the staff members. One of the nurses I was good friends with was the one who made the call.

"Erik, I'm wondering if you can help us," she said.

I hadn't forgotten the great care they had given me through all my surgeries and in the early days after I had returned from Logan. If I could help in some way, I would.

I said, "Sure, what do you need?"

"I have a patient who isn't doing so good. He's 16 years old, and he's lost all of his fingers due to frostbite."

I listened as she told me how the boy had been horrified by what had happened to his hands.

"He's 16," she went on. "You know that's an age when a zit is a major catastrophe, never mind amputation of your fingers."

I nodded. I knew only too well how the kid was feeling.

"I think he's feeling depressed," she said.

"What do you need?" I asked again.

"Well, I think if he could talk to someone who has been through what he's going through, it might help him."

"I can come over and see him. When do you want me?"

"The sooner the better; he's really bad."

I looked at my watch. It was about 11 a.m.

"Okay, I'm at work right now, but I'll try to get over there as soon as possible."

She thanked me and hung up, and I went in search of

the captain to see if I could leave right away. I explained to him what was going on and he said, "Yes, go but just check with the chief first."

It was standard procedure that I would have to go through the chain of command, so I asked the chief if I could go and help this kid who was depressed. He looked at me with what I'd come to recognize as his impatient face and said, "Sure, you can go. But not until your shift is over."

I stared at him in shock. I'd made it clear that this kid was in rough shape. I honestly did not know if he could wait until after I got off shift that night. But it was clear that the chief didn't care one iota about the boy.

I said calmly, "Okay, what is it that you would like me to work on this afternoon?"

He smiled smugly and shrugged. Then he said, "Go into the other room and read."

Anger bubbled up and threatened to spill over. He was jerking my chain, trying to get a reaction from me. If I lost my cool, it would give him something to use against me. He saw this as an opportunity to get rid of me.

I choked down my anger. I wanted my job back so I had to show that I could take commands, even when they were unjust. I reminded myself that staying calm and getting my job back would be the best way to get back at this asshole. I did what I was ordered and went in the other room and worked twice as hard.

After work I headed over to the hospital in the rush-hour traffic. I arrived around 8 p.m., two hours late.

"Hey," I said as I walked into his room.

He looked up at me and in his eyes, I recognized the

emotions running through his mind: fear, pain, hopelessness. Then he focused, first on my firefighter's uniform and then on what was left of my hands. For once, I had not tucked my hands into my pockets. I figured this kid needed to see that I had been through what he was dealing with. And I had survived and was doing just fine.

We talked for a couple of hours. He asked me a lot of questions. I told him the story of what had happened on Logan and what had happened to my hands afterward. I told him how I was getting my job back as a firefighter and how I'd started hiking again. I saw something like hope slowly fill his eyes.

"I'd like to try mountaineering," he said tentatively, almost shyly.

"As soon as you're out of here, I'll take you," I told him.

When I finally left, I felt so much better. It was the first time since my accident that I felt needed and useful. It was the first time that I realized I could actually make a difference in someone else's life.

22   Proving Myself

> *"Obstacles don't have to stop you. If you run
> into a wall, don't turn around and give up. Figure out
> how to climb it, go through it, or work around it."*
>
> —MICHAEL JORDAN

Spring 2006 – North Vancouver

Three chiefs were responsible for making sure I was qualified to get my job back. There was the chief who was not interested in helping me and who thought I was completely wasting everyone's time. The second chief was not invested one way or the other. What he cared about was whether or not I could do the job. As long as I could do what I needed to do to pass the tests, he was fine with me getting my job back.

The third chief, Chief Schreiner, saw something in me. He was not easy on me, but I think I must have intrigued him. I was so determined to get my job back, and that struck him. I used to catch him watching me with a pensive look on his face as I trained. One time I was out in the yard pulling a lanyard to raise a ladder. But my hands were so small compared to what they used to be that the motion of the exercise had to be different than before, and I just could not seem to get it. Just as I started to almost lift it, the rope would pull through my hands, and I would drop the ladder.

That day all three of the chiefs were out there watching me train, and the one who showed a desire to be rid of me just looked at me, shook his head and laughed. He walked away still laughing. The indifferent chief just mentally noted that I could not do the skill and moved on. Not judging, not laughing, but not giving me a second thought. I tried not to feel deflated when he also walked away.

Chief Schreiner's attitude toward my demonstration was different. He stood there for a long time watching. I kept trying to lift the ladder, and it kept crashing to the ground with a jarring sound. After a while, when I still could not do it, he quietly turned around and walked away, still looking pensive. Deflated, I quietly packed up the gear. I just didn't see how I could master that skill. It seemed that no matter how many times I tried, I just wasn't going to be successful.

Chief Schreiner called me to his office later that afternoon. I went right away, fear churning in my gut. I thought, "This is it. Even the guy who was somewhat on my side has had it with me." I was sure he was going to tell me that I was going to have to give up my dream. But when I got to his office he surprised me.

"I've been thinking about your problem with the lanyard, Erik."

That was a first. No one had done much more than mock me since I started training to get my job back. Here was someone actually taking an interest.

"I've been doing a bit of research," Chief Schreiner went on, "and I made a few calls."

My curiosity was piqued; I waited to see what he was going to say.

Then he said, "I think you need to invert your hand, like so." He demonstrated with his own hand. "Take the rope and make a 90° angle and try it that way."

I watched as he demonstrated a few times; excitement bubbled up. What he was saying made sense. So I went back out to the yard and tried it again. Before, with my hand straight, the rope would just pull right through. But when I inverted my hand to a 90° angle, I suddenly had resistance on the rope and it did not slide.

Doing it Chief Schreiner's way, I was able to perform the exercise easily. I got the ladder all the way to the top with the full length there. I tried it a few more times, nailing it each time, and then I noticed that he had come out to see how I was doing. He stood off to the side and watched me do it correctly a couple of times. Then he smiled, nodded to himself and walked away again without saying a word.

I suddenly felt that I actually might have someone on my side. He was not cutting me any slack, but he had not written me off just yet either. It motivated me tremendously to make him proud. To show him I could do it.

Soon after, I did the test again for all three chiefs together. Up the ladder went with no problem. I felt that the chief who had laughed at me was kind of put out that I could do it. But he could not deny that I had mastered the skill.

I thought that after proving myself to the chiefs I would automatically get my position back. But I was not reinstated so easily. Instead a representative from the Workers' Compensation Board (WCB) showed up and announced that he was required to do a report on me. He administered an arduous three-day test. Basically, he asked me to prove that I could safely use every piece of equipment on the truck.

One of the things I had to do was push and pull weight using a sled that slid along the floor on smooth running boards. The WCB tester started by asking me to push and pull 100 kilograms (220 lb) – the amount I needed to be able to move in order to pass the test. This wasn't a problem for me, so we just kept putting more weight on to see what I could do. I kept going until I'd created a record for the task at 304 kilograms (670 lb). I think it was kind of an odd situation for the WCB guy because usually he was testing people to see if they were faking injuries to get benefits. That day he had me, trying as hard as possible to prove I could do my old job. I was exerting myself on every exercise, flying through all of the tests. I could tell he was impressed.

He even took me out to a training bay and had me perform the most ridiculous things, stuff no firefighter would ever have to do, not even the rookies. For example, he asked me to cut holes above my head with a partner saw. This involved lifting the weighty saw over my head and cutting a square out of a piece of metal. This kind of activity might be part of a fire rescue, but at this stage of my career I was an officer and would never have to cut such holes. If they were needed, a junior firefighter would cut them. But in almost 20 years as a firefighter I had never actually seen anybody do it. Still, I knew I had to perform well at everything I was asked to do, so I did it. I proved I could do everything.

In the end, the WCB tester wrote a massive, positive report about me.

I felt that I'd finally accomplished what I set out to do. I had passed everything with flying colours and so I waited to get the word that I was officially back on duty. But the reluctant chief decided to accept certain portions of the report but not others.

I finally allowed myself to get mad. For months, I had done everything I could to get my job back. I had worked my butt off and finally had proved that I could do the job. Now it seemed this chief did not want me to get my job back regardless of whether I could do it or not. I started to believe that he just did not want to be proven wrong, that my success hurt his ego or something.

My union was keeping close tabs on me to see how I was doing, and at this point they stepped in. They told the department that they had to give me my job back. The department had hired me originally, I had complied with all the rules and regulations for proving that I could do the job after my injuries. If the department didn't give me my job back, the union was prepared to take legal action.

So that was that. I was allowed to return to work as a full firefighter. But that did not mean that proving myself was over. I still had to show my fellow firefighters that I could do the job. I had to prove myself on a call.

My first official call wasn't one where I could prove myself to anyone. It was a false alarm at the local high school. As is fairly standard for high-school students, someone (probably hoping to get out of a test or to play a prank) had pulled the alarm. Despite my call being a false alarm, I couldn't help feeling proud as I headed out on the firetruck. I had just come through several months of people telling me that I could not be a fireman, that my chances were slim to none and that I should not even bother trying. And I had proven them all wrong.

A week later I got my chance to really prove myself. We got a call for a crane rescue; a worker was stuck 40 metres (131 ft) up on crane, where he had apparently suffered a seizure and lost consciousness. As it turned out, I was the only one on shift who had any rope skills so I was the go-to guy. I performed the rescue.

After that nobody could question me. I had proven that not only could I do what all the other firemen could do, but I could do the job that nobody else could do, properly and safely. Since then – in April 2006, less than a year after I had been trapped on Logan – nobody has ever questioned my ability.

23 The Team and Another Mountain

"One finds limits by pushing them."

—HERBERT SIMON

June–July 2006 – Mount Elbrus

During the spring of 2006, a North Shore Rescue team was making plans to climb yet another peak: Russia's Mount Elbrus. At 5642 metres (18,511 ft), it is the highest peak in Europe and one of the Seven Summits. It had always been a mountain I wanted to climb.

I had been training so hard to get my job back that I was in pretty good shape, and a thought started to form in my head. What if I went on the Elbrus expedition? Even though I had told the press right after our rescue that I would never climb again, I knew I could not stay away from the mountains. I'd spoken under duress. Now I had a deep craving to get back into the high mountains, and my craving wasn't being satisfied on the day hikes I was doing in the Coastal Mountains.

As I'd become stronger, my day excursions had become more rigorous. I quickly moved from doing short hikes on Mount Seymour to once again going on climbs in the Tantalus Range close to my home. The healing I really needed happened in the mountains.

I don't think it occurred to anyone that I might want to go on the Elbrus expedition. It had only been a year since Logan, and after what happened there I had promised my family that I would quit climbing. But leaving my passion would not be so easy. So one night when I was out with the guys on that team I tentatively kicked around the idea of joining their team on Elbrus. They responded with a keenness that surprised me.

"You know, we could call it Team Survivor," Gord Ferguson suggested. The other guys agreed.

By now I had not only proven myself on the job front but my climbing buddies had recognized that I was determined to continue with my expeditions. I knew I wasn't quite fit for Elbrus, but I also knew I could be, and I wanted to get back on the trail. They were all supportive of my desire to join the expedition.

Some people might ask why I would want to climb again after what happened on Logan. That isn't something I can explain. I don't know if you could even say it was a want. It was more of a need. Like salmon need to spawn, I need to be on the mountain. My family was surprisingly supportive. My mom recognized that it was something I needed to do to heal. She was right. Of course, others thought I was crazy. Some of my friends questioned my wisdom in attempting a mountain like Elbrus.

Mount Elbrus is in the Caucasus Mountain Range. It is not a technical climb. It can be a long climb, but it is not a difficult one. As with Logan, weather can be a concern on Elbrus. Is it a dangerous mountain? Do people die on it? The short answer to both questions is yes. In fact, Elbrus is one of the world's deadliest mountains, with a high ratio of climber deaths to climbers. Just two years earlier, in 2004, during one climbing season 48 climbers had perished on Elbrus. But people can die on almost any mountain if the conditions are right.

The more I thought about it the more determined I was to go on this climb. My mom was right. I needed to get back in the saddle to prove to myself that I could climb again, just as I had proven that I could work as a firefighter again.

I started to make serious plans to go climb Elbrus. I upped my training to an everyday routine, hoping to regain as much of my pre-Logan fitness level as possible.

Not everyone at the fire department was happy to see me start climbing again. The reluctant chief, for example, called me into his office when he heard about my plans.

"So, Erik, I hear you are planning to go on another one of your trips?" His tone was condescending.

I smiled, which I knew would drive him nuts, "I sure am. To Mount Elbrus in Russia."

His expression hardened. "I don't think that is such a good idea. You know we have invested a lot of time and money in getting you back to work here. If you reinjure yourself on a mountain somewhere, that's just going to cause us more trouble and money down the line."

I thought to myself, "Well, you've got no problem with guys who are recreational mountain bikers or rugby players or any number of other activities that could (and often did) cause injuries." Then anger trickled in. I thought, "Who are you to tell me what I can do on my vacation time?"

Aloud I said, "Well, it is my vacation time, and I believe I have the right to do whatever I want on my own holidays."

His expression turned thunderous, but there was nothing he could do.

A few days later I got notification that my request for holiday leave had been denied. Frustrated, I went to the chief's office and asked him about it.

"Sorry, you didn't fill out your paperwork correctly so you can't have the time off," he told me.

I knew it was bullshit. I'd filled out my holiday paperwork just as I had every other time for the last 17 years. I told him as much.

"No, you didn't," he replied.

"Well, I have booked my trip already, and I won't be cancelling, so you'd better make sure my shifts are covered," I said before I left his office.

Almost immediately all my privileges at the fire hall were suspended. I wasn't stopped from going to Mount Elbrus, but I was punished. For eight months, I had no privileges, including swapping shifts with my fellow firefighters. It was the worst punishment I'd ever heard of at our hall, and it affected me greatly due to the custody arrangements with my children at the time.

The days I could spend with my children were set by the custody order so I had the kids the same days each week. I had come to rely on swapping shifts with my colleagues so that I could still drop my children off at school in the mornings and see them each week. Now that I wasn't allowed to trade shifts, I had to either see my children less or ask my ex-wife to agree to let them see me on other days. And it was all based on the fact that the chief said I did not do some paperwork properly.

Eventually, it came to light that I actually had done the paperwork correctly, but in the meantime I had to accept my lot. I refused let the negativity at work spill over into my trip plans. In fact, as the expedition to Elbrus grew closer, I became more and more excited.

There was no doubt that climbing, just like every other aspect of my life, was different without any of my fingers. Just as I'd had to learn to do things differently at the fire hall, I needed to relearn how to use my climbing gear. I chose not to use adapted gear. I just adjusted how I used what I had always used.

I could not have picked a better team to go with. The NSR members were my family. They looked out for me on the mountain. They wanted me to succeed as much as I wanted to. There were five of us on what we dubbed Team Survivor. Two members, besides me, were from the 2005 Logan team: Ales Ponec and Gord Ferguson. The other two members were Karl Winters, an accomplished mountaineer, and Greg Miller, a long-time NSR member and experienced climber.

We started the trip by staying in Ales's home village of Spindleruv Mlyn in the mountains of the Czech Republic, getting in shape with hiking and drinking slivovitz (plum brandy). Then Team Survivor continued to Moscow and boarded a 1970s-era Turkorov passenger jet for a flight – maybe more dangerous than the one to Logan – to the climbers' entry point of Mineralnye Vody in the Caucasus Mountains.

While we were there the local rescue team was still searching the peak for a group of climbers that had gone missing and died during a summit attempt before we arrived. No sign of their fate had been found. Their plight certainly highlights the big difference conditions can make relative to success, failure or disaster in the mountains

We left Base Camp on Elbrus on June 27, 2006, and, unlike on Logan, we had perfect conditions. We summited on Canada Day 2006 (July 1), just over 13 months after the Logan disaster.

On the way up the mountain, it became apparent to me pretty quickly that I was not in the same shape as the rest of the team. Despite my daily training regime at home, months in the hospital had taken their toll. I was able to keep up with them, but just barely. When I did fall behind, the guys kept an eye out for me without making a big deal out of it.

At one point, we were climbing with our crampons on. The rest of the team was climbing ahead of me when one of my crampons came off. I sat down and struggled to get it back on my foot, but despite my best efforts, I was not able to refasten it. Frustration swept over me, and I was ready to give up, when Greg Miller suddenly sat down beside me.

Without saying a word, he reached over and refastened the crampon. Then he turned and started climbing again as if nothing had happened.

I looked up at his back and felt nothing more than gratitude and appreciation for the dedicated individuals I was climbing with. Not once did they make me feel that I was less of a team member. I wasn't coddled or treated any differently than anyone else. When I couldn't do something, one of my teammates would react in the same manner Greg had: quietly and without any fanfare or fuss, usually without words.

I was slower than the rest of the team, and I was the last to reach the summit on Canada Day. We all stood on the summit together for a few photos and congratulations, and then the rest of the team started down and left me on my own to ponder the accomplishment.

It was the best feeling in the world standing on the highest peak in Europe on Canada Day and feeling like I had my life back. I just stood there, looking around and giving thanks for that life.

It was a different life but it was my life. I thought about how far I had come since Mount Logan. I tried to remember the man I had been when I set off a little more than a year earlier for Yukon, and I found I barely recognized that individual. I had been changed in more than just physical ways by what had happened on that mountain. For example, I had developed a far deeper appreciation for the gift of life since Logan. I had lost a lot in 2005, but I had gained so much from the experience. I'm not going to lie and say that what I had gained was worth losing my fingers for, but

I had come to a place of peace with what had happened. It happened. And I had to accept that.

As I stood in the sunshine atop Elbrus I suddenly realized that I truly had accepted what had happened to me. I wasn't scared anymore. I knew that the human spirit is far stronger than we typically give it credit for. I had surprised everyone, including myself, with what I had achieved, and I knew that putting limits on what I could do was the surest pathway to failure.

As Dr. O'Malley in Alaska had told me, the only one who would determine what I could or could not do in my life was myself. And I didn't really believe in limits.

Before I left the summit, I deposited the small plastic bag containing my children's pictures – this time pictures of three children: Shayman, Ariyah and Joline.

The rest of my team had continued down to Base Camp without me. I think they were giving me space to contemplate what this summit meant to me. I didn't hurry down; I couldn't have, anyway. The summit had exhausted me physically and mentally. I felt as though I were carrying ten-pound cinder blocks on each of my feet as I descended. I was so thoroughly wasted. But I was grateful for the quiet time to reflect and think about my life. I knew that if I ran into trouble, my team was just a radio call away.

I had shown that I could accomplish what I set out to do. I had got my job back; I had summited the highest peak in Europe. I had done it all with no fingers. I had proven what I was capable of to my family, my colleagues, and my friends: all the naysayers and all the supporters. But most of all I had proven it to myself. I could do it. It made me believe I could do anything. I could move ahead with my life.

As I soloed down, I thought of all the things I'd done, all the places I'd been, and I started to dream of all the things I would do in the future. The possibilities now seemed almost endless. I wondered what other challenges and adventures my life would bring me. I knew now that mountaineering would always be a vital part of my life. I thought of all the peaks I'd attempted: in Africa, Europe, North America, South America and Asia. Everest floated through my mind, as it had done so many times before Logan.

Everest would be a great challenge for me. Suddenly I knew: "One day. Everest will be a mountain I will climb." With that affirmation settled, I descended from Elbrus, a bright future beckoning.

Donating to North Shore Rescue

If you enjoyed this book, please consider making a donation of either time or money to your local search and rescue team. Most rescue teams are made up of volunteers and are run on donations from the public. The brave men and women who have joined these teams to bolster their communities and share their skills are often called on for the ultimate sacrifice.

You never know when you or your loved ones may need these dedicated individuals on your side.

North Shore Rescue is one of the oldest SAR teams in the country and relies on donations to carry out their important work. Donations to North Shore Rescue can be made online at: https://www.canadahelps.org/en/charities/north-shore-search-and-rescue-vancouver-sr-team/. You can also contact the team at http://northshorerescue.com.

Appendix A

Chronology of Events

May 1, 2005	Leave North Vancouver
May 2	Overnight in Smithers, BC
May 3	Arrive at Haines Junction, Yukon
May 5	Fly to Base Camp
May 6–10	Build Base Camp and set up camps en route to the summit
May 11–15	Storm at King Col
May 22	Arrive at Plateau Camp
May 23	Barry Mason, Mike Danks and Gord Ferguson go for summit bid; Barry Mason successfully summits Mount Logan
May 24	Isabel Budke and Erik attempt the summit
May 25	13:00 – Erik, Don Jardine and Alex Snigurowicz begin descent from Advance Camp
	16:00 – Storm hits team on Prospector Col; take shelter in tent
May 26	12:00 – Lose tent to the storm
	18:00 – Don and Alex take Erik to snow cave

May 27	04:00 – Storm subsides
	07:00 – Erik, Don and Alex make contact with Gord Ferguson
	11:00 – Gord and Linda Bily arrive at Prospector Col
	18:00 – First helicopters arrive
	23:00 – Jim Hood lifts Erik off the mountain
May 28	01:00 – Alex and Don lifted off mountain
	04:00 – Erik, Don and Alex transported to Anchorage
May 28–June 1	Recovery in Anchorage
June 1	Return to Vancouver
Summer	Hospitalization and multiple surgeries
Fall	Recovery, rehabilitation and training
April 2006	Passes tests and goes back to firefighting
July 1, 2006	Erik and North Shore Rescue Team summit Mount Elbrus

Appendix B

Camps on Logan

Base Camp (Quintino Sella Glacier) – 2750 metres (9,000 ft)

Camp 2 (King's Trench) – 3365 metres (11,000 ft)

Camp 3 (King Col) – 4095 metres (13,500 ft)

Camp 4 (Football Field) – 4500 metres (14,850 ft)

Camp 5 – 4900 metres (16,200 ft)

Camp 6 (Plateau Main Camp) – 5200 metres (17,600 ft)

Camp 7 (Plateau Advance camp) – 5200 metres (17,600 ft)

Bibliography

Arnold, Kevin. "Two Mountains to Climb." *The Globe and Mail*. July 27, 2002. T7.

Austin, Ian. "High-Level Rescue: Sharp Reflexes Save Worker from Deadly Fall." *The Province*. May 19, 2006. A30.

"Back on the Job." *North Shore Outlook*. June 8, 2006. 14.

Baddelt, Brad, and Miller, Jennifer. "'I've Never Seen a Storm Hit Like That': Climber to Lose Fingers to Frostbite." *National Post*. May 30, 2005. A7.

———. "Logan Climbers Rescued: 'I thought I was dead.'" *Vancouver Sun*. May 30, 2005. A1.

Baron, Ethan. "B.C. Trio Survive Mount Logan Storm." *The Gazette*. May 29, 2005. A1.

———. "Climbers Plucked from Mt. Logan: Mountaineers frostbitten but Glad to be Alive after Storm." *Calgary Herald*. May 29, 2005. A3.

———. "Climbers Recount Frigid Ordeal on Canada's Highest Mountain." *Times-Colonist*. May 29, 2005. A4.

———. "Mountaineers Survive Logan Ordeal." *The Province*. May 29, 2005. A3.

"B.C. Climber Gets Trapped on Mountain." *The Westcoast Reader*. September 2005. 1.

"B.C. Search Leader's Emotions Involved in Rescue of Three Climbers." *Daily Bulletin*. May 31, 2005. 12.

Beddall, Justin. "A Team to the End." *North Shore Outlook*. June 2, 2005. 1.

———. "Conquering the Next Mountain." *North Shore Outlook*. July 7, 2005. 3.

————. "The Best Christmas Gift Ever." *North Shore Outlook.* December 22, 2005. 12.

————. "A Firefighter Hands Down." *North Shore Outlook.* June 8, 2006. 1.

————."Experiencing Life." *North Shore Outlook.* September 20, 2007. 7.

Boukreev, Anatoli. *Above the Clouds: The Diaries of a High-Altitude Mountaineer.* New York: St. Martin's Griffin, 2002. 31.

Buhl, Herman. "Climb Report: Quotes." http://climbreport. net/quotes/.

"Canadian Climber Dies on Mount Logan." *Seattle Times.* June 11, 2005.

Carnegie Hero Fund Commission. "James P. Hood." http:// www.carnegiehero.org/awardees/profiles/hood/.

Carrigg, David. "Mt. Logan Climber Reunited with his Family: Fireman Will Lose Tips of his Fingers." *The Province.* June 3, 2005. A30.

CBC Television. *The National.* June 3, 2005. Segment 005.

Chu, Richard. "Rescuers Battled Fatigue, Snow to Reach 3 Climbers." *Vancouver Sun.* June 4, 2005. B4.

"Climbers Barely Escape Fierce Storm." *Trail Times.* May 30, 2005. 2.

"Climbers Return to Families in Vancouver." *The Whitehorse Star.* June 3, 2005. 4.

"Editorial: Firefighter Grabs Life by the Horns." *North Shore Outlook.* June 8, 2006. 8.

Eliot, T.S. "Preface." In *Transit of Venus: Poems* by Harry Crosby. Paris: Black Sun Press, 1931.

"From Despair to 'Elation.'" *The Leader.* June 8, 2005. 1.

Government of Yukon. "Mount Logan: Canadian Titan. Virtual Museums." 2007. http://www.virtualmuseum.ca/sgc-cms/expositions-exhibitions/logan/en/index.php?/md/Home.

Greg, Erin. "Quadriplegic Climbs over Kilimanjaro: North Vancouver Resident Aided by Five Porters as He Attains World Record." *Vancouver Sun.* August 31, 2002. B9.

Hansen, Rick. "Community Heroes." January 14, 2012. http://myhero.com/hero.asp?hero=R_Hansen_dnhs_US_2012.

"High-Altitude Helicopter Key to Saving Mountaineers." *Trail Times.* May 31, 2005. 2.

Hillary, Edmund. "Conqueror of Mt. Everest." http://www.siredmundhillary.com/hillary.htm.

Holdsworth, Gerald. "Mount Logan, Vol. 1." *Arctic Institute of North America.* 2000.

Hunter, Stuart. "Climber Gets his Life, and his Daughter: Happy Ending for Rescued B.C. Man." *Ottawa Citizen.* June 5, 2005. A5.

———."Stranded Climber May Lose Fingers but He's Regained a Lost Daughter." *Edmonton Journal.* June 5, 2005. A9.

———. "Reunion Awaits Hospitalized Climber." *Calgary Herald.* June 5, 2005. A2.

———. "Hospitalized Mountaineer Says He Will Soon Be Reunited with Long-Lost Daughter." *National Post.* June 6, 2005. A10.

Jobs, Steve. "Stanford Commencement Address." 2005. https://news.stanford.edu/2005/06/14/jobs-061505/.

Jordan, Michael. "10 Amazing Success Lessons from Michael Jordan." October 14, 2010. http://www.pickthebrain.com/blog/10-amazing-success-lessons-from-michael-jordan/.

Kukuczka, Jerzy. *My Vertical World: Climbing the 8000-Metre Peaks.* Seattle: Mountaineers Books, 1992.

Labelle, Joseph C. "Life and Research at 5,311 Meters, Mount Logan, Yukon: Physiology Studies." *Mountain Research and Development* 16, no. 3 (1996): 313.

Lambart, H.F. "The Conquest of Mount Logan." *The Geographical Journal*, LXVIII, no. 1 (July 1926): 1–23.

Lamott, Anne. *Traveling Mercies: Some Thoughts on Faith.* New York: Anchor Books, 2001. 143.

Lazaruk, Susan. "Father, Daughter United: Mount Logan Climber Who Cheated Death Meets Child He Never Knew." *The Province.* June 7, 2005. A10.

Loewen, Bree. *Pickets and Dead Men: Seasons on Rainier.* Seattle: Mountaineers Books, 2009.

Lowe, Alex. "Climbing Quotes." http://winterclimb.com/articles/item/1-climbing-quotes.

Luymes, Glenda. "I May Lose My Hands, but I Can Still Hold My Kids." *Edmonton Journal.* May 30, 2005. A5.

———. "Mount Logan Rescuers Arrive Safely at Base Camp." *The Province.* June 1, 2005, A11.

Macfarlane, Robert. *Mountains of the Mind: A History of a Fascination.* London: Granta Books, 2008.

Madgic, Bob. *Shattered Air: A True Account of Catastrophe and Courage on Yosemite's Half Dome.* New York: Burford Books, 2007.

Mandela, Nelson. "Nelson Mandela's Legacy for Climate Hawks: 'It Always Seems Impossible Until It's Done.'" December 6, 2013. http://thinkprogress.org/climate/2013/12/06/3031231/nelson-mandelas-legacy-climate-hawks/.

"May Lose Fingers but at Least He's Alive." *Peace River Block Daily News.* May 30, 2005. 2.

McPhee, Erin. "Climbers Share in Recovery." *North Shore News.* July 31, 2005. 3.

Messner, Reinhold. *All Fourteen 8,oooers.* Seattle: Mountaineers Books, 1999.

———. "Quotes." https://terrainterminate.wordpress.com/quotes/.

Michaud, Deneka. "Mountain Rescuer Awarded: Gord Ferguson Saved Three on Mount Logan." *North Shore News.* August 4, 2006. 5.

Moore, G.W.K., and Gerald Holdsworth. "The 25–27 May 2005 Mount Logan Storm. Part I: Observations and Synoptic Overview." *Journal of Hydrometeorology* 8 (2007): 590–606.

Moore, G.W.K., and J.L. Semple. "Freezing and Frostbite on Mount Everest: New Insights into Wind Chill and Freezing Times at Extreme Altitude." *High Altitude Medicine & Biology* (2011).

"Mount Logan Survivors Recuperating after Ordeal." *The Globe and Mail.* May 31, 2005. A7.

O'Connor, Elaine. "Rescued Climber Rebuilds Life: North Van Man Finds Family, Mends Rifts, Awaits Work." *The Province.* December 16, 2005. A4.

Pang, Yumimi. "Climber Back on Top: After Losing Nine Fingers, Mountain-High Goals Motivate Firefighter." *The Province.* July 31, 2006. A12.

———. "You Can't Keep a Good Firefighter Down: Bjarnason Hitting the Peaks Again." *North Shore News.* August 16, 2006. 3.

Pfisterer, Willy. "Funny Climbing Quotes." July 6, 2009. http://blog.alpineinstitute.com/2009/07/funny-climbing-quotes.html.

Read, Nicholas. "Injured Climber Eyes Everest: Series: Summer Conversations." *Vancouver Sun.* July 8, 2005. B2.

"Rescue Members Reach Safety of Base Camp." *Nanaimo Daily News.* June 1, 2005. A5.

Schuller, Robert H. *Tough Times Never Last, but Tough People Do!* New York: Bantam, 1984.

Seyd, Jane. "Rescue Team Members Face Death: Trek on Canada's Highest Peak Ends in Dramatic Retrieval." *North Shore News.* June 1, 2005. 1.

———. "Frostbitten Hikers Treated at VGH." *North Shore News.* June 5, 2005. 1.

Simon, Herbert. "One Finds Limits by Pushing Them." October 20, 2012. http://www.barrypopik.com/index.php/new_york_city/entry/one_finds_limits_by_pushing_them.

Simpson, Joe. *Touching the Void: The True Story of One Man's Miraculous Survival.* New York: Harper Perennial, 1988.

Stall, Bob. "Leaving No Stones Unturned." *The Province.* March 22, 1996. A8.

"Stranded Climber Meets Daughter for First Time." *Kamloops Daily News.* June 8, 2005. B4.

"Three Men Where [sic] Were Trapped on Mount Logan Return Home to Vancouver." *The Canadian Press Newswire.* June 3, 2005.

"Trapped B.C. Climber Wrote Goodbye Note to family." *Daily Press.* May 30, 2005. A6.

"Trapped Climbers Survive Brutal Storm atop Peak." *The Record.* May 30, 2005. C12.

Tzu, Lao. "When I let Go of What I am, I Become what I Might Be." http://philosiblog.com/2012/07/19/when-i-let-go-of-what-i-am-i-become-what-i-might-be/.

Viesturs, Edmund, and David Roberts. *No Shortcut to the Top: Climbing the World's 14 Highest Peaks*. New York: Broadway Books, 2006.

Walton, Dawn. "Stranded Climbers Were Just Hours from Death." *The Globe and Mail*. May 30, 2005. A1.

Waterman, Jon. "Great Mountains of the World: Mt. Logan." *Adventure Journal*. https://adventure-journal.com/2012/07/great-mountains-of-the-world-mt-logan-2/.

"You Said It." *North Shore News*. June 5, 2005. 6.

"You Said It." *North Shore News*. August 20, 2006. 6.

Index